Keeper Tales
of Training
with
Positive Reinforcement

ZOOmility

BY GREY STAFFORD, PhD

An iReinforce.com Book

ZO(m)ility

Keeper Tales of Training with Positive Reinforcement

An iReinforce.com Book

Library of Congress Control Number: 2007929349
ISBN 978-0-979681-00-4

Printed in the United States of America

Give her the reward she has earned,
and let her works bring her praise...
                              -Proverbs 31:31

TABLE OF CONTENTS

PART TWO

But *My* Walrus Isn't a Clean Slate

FOREWORD

Animals—what a wonderful part of our lives, whether they're elephants, bears, gorillas, tigers, or pandas still living in the wild, or the dogs, cats, birds, or hamsters that share our homes! I can't imagine a life without the enrichment provided by our furry, feathery, or scaly friends.

But all too often, we think of our pets as existing exclusively for our enjoyment. Indeed, pets are animals. But they are also individuals with important lives, as well as specific needs and desires that we should learn more about. Our pets provide us great enjoyment. In return, we owe them more attention than some of us typically give. Not just the usual pat-on-the-head attention, but also the kind that will foster a better relationship between pet and pet "keeper." We need to learn what makes them tick.

Unfortunately, in addition to being cute and cuddly, a lot of our furry companions have bad habits. The problem is that we usually tolerate these undesirable behaviors so long as our pets satisfy us by jumping up in our laps, playing with us, or sleeping at the foot of the bed. We may try our best to discipline—maybe offering a stern "no, no" in the hope that the unwanted behaviors will disappear. But they don't.

OK. You just caught Rover in the act of chewing the leg of your expensive end table. You reprimand him with whatever style you use. The problem? Most animals can't connect what they did that their owner doesn't like with the punishment they've just received. All they know is that their owner acted really mean to them for no apparent reason! Needless to say, for creatures that don't process information quite like we humans, they become very confused!

Our pets deserve proper training so that we can develop mutually beneficial, healthy, and happy relationships. No one wants pets that are afraid of their owner, or afraid of new people, places, and things! All this sounds well and good, right? But how do you achieve a brand new relationship with your pet? Read on and you'll find out!

For decades, marine mammal trainers like Dr. Grey Stafford have developed and perfected techniques to teach whales and dolphins some amazing behaviors—not by force, but with mutual trust and cooperation based on the principles of positive reinforcement. Can you imagine how difficult it would be to train one of these creatures? Sure they're intelligent, but they live in a very different environment than your dog or cat.

You can sit in your comfortable living room and try to teach Rover to sit. For the most part, you're in control of the situation. If he loses interest, he may run into another room. But you can follow him and resume your training session. This is not true for trainers working with animals that swim deep in the sea, or for that matter, those that fly high in the sky, swing from the tallest trees, or run in large herds across the plains.

So how does a successful trainer get the animal's attention and hold it long enough to teach any behavior, let alone a complex one? Marine mammal trainers have faced numerous difficulties and they've developed successful techniques to overcome these challenges. Transferring these training tips to any zoo or domestic animal is the key...and it works!

I first met Grey back in the early 90's when he was just starting his zoological career working with marine mammals. Since then, his work in zoos, oceanariums, and television has enabled him to apply those same principles of reinforcement training to dozens of exotic and endangered species. Along the way, he's helped many pet owners and professionals provide better care for their animals through positive reinforcement.

So I invite you to invest some time and energy into studying these techniques. When you apply them to your own animals, you'll begin to enjoy a much better life for both you and your sidekick!

Jack Hanna
Director Emeritus, Columbus Zoo
Host, Jack Hanna's TV series

Acknowledgements

John Donne wrote, "No man is an island" and that certainly describes my life. For as long as I can remember, my family has always been in my corner. In fact, raising two kids by herself and often opening our home to anyone in need, my mother set the standard for putting the interests of others above her own—perhaps my first and best lesson in zoomility.

I am so grateful for the amazing opportunities that have come my way to care for, study, train, and present so many different species to the public. Those lessons, as well as the many people, not all of whom can be listed, who have shared their time and knowledge with me, have made *Zoomility* a reality. As every author knows, producing a book is a lengthy and technical process. For their work, helpful advice, and friendship I want to thank Terry Samansky, Lee Hill, Peter Mortimer, Gary Bennett, Jennifer Nichols, Dave Owens, Kim Strollo, Traci Terrible, Dr. James Blank, Dr. Kim Nguyen, and Denise DeWitt.

I am indebted to Debbie and Glenn Hotze for being the first to open my eyes to the dire state of pet training that existed not all that long ago. They turned to reinforcement-only training before it was the "in" thing to do. As a result, few people have sacrificed as much personally and professionally, while trying to help desperate animals get their owners away from the heavy hand of punishment, as those two have.

Thanks to all my colleagues at SeaWorld, past and present, including Thad Lacinak, Chuck Tompkins, Stewart Clark, Jim Nemet, and Julie Scardina; in particular, Ted Turner for helping to make my animal training career possible. To the extraordinary people at Dolphin Quest, I could not have done this without you or our "boys." Your dedication to ensuring that every animal succeeds inspires me still. I want to thank the great staff at Wildlife World Zoo, especially Mickey Ollson, zoo director and founder, for the trust he has shown me. While many people dream of building their own accredited zoo and aquarium, he actually accomplished it. I also want to express my gratitude to Rick Prebeg and Kate Oliphint from the Columbus Zoo.

Special thanks goes to Jungle Jack Hanna, one of the nicest and most generous people you'd ever want to meet. Many of us dedicated to the important work occurring in accredited zoos and aquariums everywhere would consider ourselves lucky to contribute even one tenth of what he and his family have done to promote conservation of wildlife and wild places. Jack's *Animal Adventures* television show has raised public awareness about our planet and inspired generations of future zookeepers. I am honored by his contribution to this book.

Finally, I want to thank my wife, Karen, whose unwavering support and sacrifices have enabled me to write this book and to do the work I love.

INTRODUCTION

A well-timed story, phrase, or even a few simple words passed on from mentor to student can dramatically alter a person's life, both personally and professionally. Instead of passing into oblivion, like so many other early memories, these powerful ideas build within us, solidify, and help form the basis for everything that follows–often by surprise without any conscious effort. And so it has been for me, ever since I heard a mentor's impassioned plea to "teach our animals to be winners." This was no faint-hearted attempt to motivate an overworked dolphin training staff performing in front of thousands on a hot summer day. Rather, it was a call to action and a challenge to us to make our animals, not our egos, the number one priority. Accepting the challenge meant changing our ingrained thinking from brooding about and reacting to the mistakes our animals made, to positively reinforcing all their successful behaviors that until then, we frequently took for granted. Perhaps that's why whenever the opportunity to assist other trainers comes along, regardless of the species, I find myself repeating his sage words about the importance of doing whatever we can to help animals succeed in the environment we've created for them.

It doesn't matter whether these people are working with dogs, dolphins, or donkeys. Lasting progress can only happen once we give up the urge to repeatedly say "No!" to mistakes in favor of looking for ways to say "Yes!" to their successful behaviors. Furthermore, positive reinforcement training frees us from the trap of inflicting pain and fear through punishment on the very animals we care for and respect. It grants us the freedom to give animals access to the things they need and desire—most of all, it allows us to show them our love and affection! For when we succeed at teaching animals "Yes, good job," there's no need to also point out their mistakes with punishment. The reason? Animals that get better at achieving success necessarily get worse at attaining failure.

To this day, the lessons learned from a career focused on animals are helpful personal reminders whenever I start taking my own training sessions, or myself, too seriously. Don't get me wrong. The art and science of training behaviors is serious business whether it takes place in a zoo or the home. For example, zoos and aquariums are increasingly teaching wild and potentially dangerous animals how to safely participate in their own survival, in cooperation with their human caretakers. Ultimately, the growing trend of zoos using positive reinforcement training to enhance the lives of individual animals may also help prevent the extinction of entire species. So too, in our homes, having a successful pet means a better and longer life for every member of the family! However, pet owners and animal professionals of all types can get caught up in the moment by placing way too much value on a single training session, a few successful approximations or, heaven forbid, a few mistakes. The reality of animal learning is, it almost always takes more than one successful attempt to teach a desired behavior. But the good news is, it usually takes more than one poor training session to break it. The key to making steady improvement is to avoid overreacting to failure or growing overconfident from a little progress.

Like many zookeepers I suppose, not all of my teachers have been human. In fact, the more time I spend around animals, wild or domestic, the more I am awed by their ability to adapt to changing circumstances. Behavior is perhaps the most flexible attribute of all living creatures. Yet through our own arrogance, human expectations often box the animals we work with into finite roles capable of only a limited set of behavioral responses. I wish I had that proverbial nickel for every time I've heard someone blame a creature's "instinct" as the cause of unwanted behavior, like aggression, rather than his or her own poor training practices! Physical characteristics may take several generations of animals to alter. But an animal's ability to learn from changing conditions is far greater than many of us realize. This is not to suggest that pigs will one day learn to fly, since they lack the basic machinery to engage in such behaviors. But in general, animals can learn to cope with all sorts of changes to their environment. They'd better. Human activities are transforming the world so dramatically and in ways we may never fully appreciate, that the survival of many species will rely, in part, on their ability to *behaviorally* adjust to the rapid pace of global change. For those of you concerned with helping the animals in your own lives, the take home lesson is this: when it comes to what any animal can learn with positive reinforcement, the sky truly is the limit. So don't be quick to lay blame for their behavior problems on genetics!

Still, why should you pay attention to the ideas found in this book? No doubt for some animal trainers, keepers, and pet owners, the axiom "talk is cheap" easily comes to mind. In my experience, people who are passionate about animals can be a tough group to convince unless they see or do it themselves, and rightly so. The proof of success should be in the results. And the results of positive reinforcement training are there if you know where to look. In accredited zoos and aquariums everywhere, keepers are using the behavior tools that marine mammal trainers have honed for decades to positively reinforce all sorts of useful, complex, and cooperative behaviors with birds, mammals, reptiles, and even fish! The great news is, the tools described here are easy to learn and will work with your animals too, regardless of species or breed.

> **Try not to let your preconceived notions or past unsuccessful training experiences with a species, breed, or individual limit what you think they can or cannot learn in the future.**[1]

When you train using only positive reinforcement, the richer life you and your animal will experience together far outweighs any initial investment in time, patience, and energy used to *modify your own behavior*. Plus, aside from all the rational arguments supporting the use of this thing called positive reinforcement as a way to teach your animal, the most obvious reason is, it's fun! As you begin to see your animal succeed, you too will get plenty of reinforcement of your own. And isn't that one of the reasons we live, work, study, or play around animals anyway? Intrigued? I hope so. For the skeptics, read on, keep an open mind, and when you're finished, if need be, prove me wrong.

What is Zoomility?

First, let's try to find common ground by considering a simple truth revealed to me by a litany of humbling and often public mistakes that happened while working in a zoo: ***good training decisions usually start with leaving your ego at the door***. For my part, each chapter of this book begins with some personal tales of zookeeper humility or "zoomility." Done properly, training is as much about having fun as it is about helping animals succeed in the world in which we've placed them, whether it be a zoo, a kennel, a wildlife preserve, a stable, or our own home. Behavior training should be all about what the animals need in order to thrive. Selfish, lazy, uptight, or impatient trainers often fail both themselves and their animals. They simply lack zoomility.

So this book was written to provide readers useful training tips as well as a glimpse at the funny side of working around animals with positive reinforcement. Hopefully, finding a little humor in some of my mistakes will help you to avoid anger and frustration in your own training situations, to resist applying punishment to "correct" behaviors, and most of all, to embrace the joy of training through positive reinforcement. Learning to put aside your own training ego and adopting a little zoomility will help you build a healthier, more dependable, and more successful relationship with your animal students, whatever species they may be.

Since not all animals have the same training history, *Zoomility* is divided into two parts. The first begins with a discussion of the superior benefits of training without using force and punishment. It highlights the fundamental difference between punishment trainers, those who focus on mistakes, and reinforcement trainers who, by definition, focus on behavioral success. It also addresses the basic process by which all animals seem to learn. Readers are encouraged to model their training methods after this natural learning process by using the 3R's: Request, Response, and Reinforce. Using the 3R's, trainers can expect to build higher criteria behaviors and a stronger relationship with their animal— one that is based upon mutual trust, not fear. This first half of *Zoomility* is ideally suited to any animal professional or pet owner who is just starting out with young or naïve animals. I call these animals the "clean slates" that have not yet learned a strong set of undesirable behaviors. This section concludes with several useful behavior "recipes" to help readers get started training with zoomility in their own homes. Each recipe takes the behavior to be trained and breaks it down into simpler steps in order to clarify the principles discussed.

The second part of *Zoomility* is aimed at helping those of us with animals that have experienced a few training mistakes along the way, whether at our own hands or the hands of others, including training with punishment. This section can also help those of us who have inherited an animal with an unknown or unpleasant training history. Part two begins with some tips on how owners can remain reinforcement-only trainers even when animals display unwanted behaviors. The goal is to help readers avoid the temptation of applying punishment even in the face of undesirable behaviors, including aggression.

Zoomility concludes with a detailed look at one of several dolphins I was lucky to work with in my career. As with so many other creatures, this animal's training history had been a "mixed bag" of methods, environments, behavior expectations, trainer experience, and most of all, serious aggression towards humans. From the moment he joined our all male dolphin collection, this animal proved to be one of the biggest training challenges and one of the greatest learning opportunities of my life. His story highlights the amazing improvements that can be achieved with a deliberate and carefully executed behavioral plan using only positive reinforcement. It

13

also serves as a reminder and motivator to all of us that it is much easier to prevent behavior problems from taking hold than it is to repair them once learned, even when the solutions are based only on reinforcement. By the end of this book, readers will possess the knowledge to use positive reinforcement to assess and create conditions that will ensure their animals will be more successful in the future.

A Few Words About Terminology

A useful book about training should probably also include a little training terminology. For years, I've heard people from all walks of life complain about the overuse of behavioral jargon and the under-use of concrete, real-life examples in training discussions. I think much of this criticism is justified. Instead of getting down to the heart of the matter, some authors and consultants have tended to complicate things with obscure, unnecessary, or even worse, inaccurate and unsubstantiated terms! This problem is real and leads to greater confusion, particularly among new pet owners. For example, many people, even training instructors, interchangeably use the terms *punishment* and *negative reinforcement* despite the fact that these consequences have completely opposite effects on behavior: punishment suppresses the preceding behavior, while negative reinforcement encourages it. Yet even with their initial complexity, overuse, or misuse, certain behavioral terms, when accurately defined, are vital for the effective and efficient training of animals as well as for sharing that knowledge with others. So, while every effort will be made to use only the most relevant behavioral terms and definitions, this book discusses fundamental concepts wherever appropriate with the hope that the reader will become familiar and fluent with these terms. For further reading, cited materials and additional references with behavior glossaries are listed at the end of the book. And with that, it's time to see why your animals will have healthier and more successful lives when you train with zoomility using only positive reinforcement!

PART ONE

A Clean Slate

How was your first
day of work,
dear?

ZOOMILITY 101

No matter what training mistakes you may have made in the past, I'm willing to bet that mine are equally bad if not worse. So you shouldn't let your past failures hold you back from becoming a reinforcement trainer. Don't believe me? Well, consider my first day on the job at a new zoo.

Several years ago, I was hired to manage a zoo's education department and program animal collection. I started during the normally slow summer season in Phoenix when the department always slims down to just full-time staff. As luck would have it, the full timers had all moved on to new zoos. So from day one, I was on my own to meet, assess, and care for the trained animals—including about a dozen free flight show birds. With years of experience in animal training under my belt, I was confident I could teach these animals some great behaviors.

One of those animals was Domingo, a two-year-old green wing macaw. Like the rest of the large birds behind stage that first morning, Domingo sat on his perch at the back of his enclosure, eyeing my every move as I washed and filled water bowls. When it came time to enter his walk-in habitat, I slowly cracked the door open just far enough to slip myself through but not enough for him to take flight through the doorway. Or so I thought. Having worked mostly with big creatures like whales and sea lions up to that point, I had no idea a macaw could fly through a 12-inch gap! Domingo never looked back. The last I saw of him, he was heading past the southern end of the zoo on his way to

17

who knows where.

I spent the rest of the day and evening in a futile attempt to find him on the zoo's heavily treed 50-acre grounds. Fortunately for me, the zoo director was willing to let me come back a second day to try and make amends for losing a valuable tropical bird in the hot Arizona desert.

The next day, tired and a little thirsty, Domingo showed up and allowed me to keep my job. Apparently, as I later learned, he had been rehearsing this behavior for some time and I was his latest victim. Talk about a lesson in zoomility.

Why Teach with Only Positive Reinforcement?

Training is about relationships. Clearly, on that first day and for a little while after that, Domingo and I didn't have a good relationship. The question remaining was whether a good relationship was even possible between that bird so adept at flying away and me. More importantly, what would be the basis of that relationship?

That same question has to be answered in every human/animal relationship. Whether you're a new pet owner or an experienced animal handler, trainer, keeper, or health care professional, the most important question you have to ask yourself before you even get near an animal is "do I want our relationship to be based on mutual trust or fear?" When the outcome matters—when it really counts whether your animal is successful or not—do you think to yourself, "I want this animal to trust me" or conversely, "I want this animal to be afraid of me"? Keep in mind that sugarcoating the word *fear* by calling it *respect* doesn't fundamentally change a relationship based on intimidation backed up by force. In dealing with animals, those are the options—fear or trust.

If you're not sure which to choose, consider a different kind of animal. Most people never have the chance to train anything other than your typical domestic pet. But what if you could? Rather than thinking about a small, eager-to-please animal that's easy to physically dominate, imagine yourself face to face with one of the biggest animals on the planet, like an African elephant. Would you change your answer knowing that one misstep by the elephant (or you) could end with your body being hurled across the paddock, bones snapped in two? Or what if you were facing the fastest animal—the cheetah? Which training method would you choose knowing you could easily be outrun at any moment by a cunning predator? And consider the other side—what if you were facing a naturally fearful animal such as a gazelle? Sure, you'll have no trouble intimidating this species. But the delicate gazelle's natural defenses might also cause it to run blindly away from the sound of your approaching footsteps, oblivious to any deadly barriers present that could cause instant death.

The bottom line? You can't push an elephant around.

After imagining yourself in those situations, if you still prefer a relationship based upon fear, then put this book back on the shelf. It's not for you. Whether in a home, a zoo, a pet shelter, a horse stable, or anywhere humans and animals coexist, if you are searching for a better and more fun-filled way to help animals be more successful, then read on!

In essence, *you* must choose. Will you be a punishment trainer, always reacting to mistakes? Or will you be a reinforcement trainer, responding to an animal's successes? For their part, pets don't have much of a say in how caretakers choose to train them. To them, each day is a struggle to gain reinforcement and avoid punishment, whether it comes from you or the environment.

Like me, many of you may have grown up conditioned to believe you must correct or punish unwanted behavior if you want to quickly and efficiently train your pet. But does training with punishment really lead to faster, better, and longer lasting results? As my early zoo experience soon taught me, the answer is no. In actuality, training with punishment is very inefficient! Teaching an animal, "No, that's not the right thing to do" is not the same as teaching, "Yes! Please do this." While punishment may reduce the likelihood that certain behaviors will be displayed again in the future, it does nothing to communicate what behaviors the trainer really wants to see.

What should a punished animal do now? And what should it have done to avoid punishment in the first place? Training with punishment doesn't answer either of these basic questions. As a result, trainers focused on catching their animals making mistakes can spend a lifetime teaching an animal what not to do. And in the end, there's no guarantee the animal will ever know what it should do to be successful. Life is too short to spend every waking minute shouting "No," "Cht," "Wrong," "Bad dog," or "STOP!" and hoping the animal will figure out the rest on its own.

By now I hope it's clear that using positive reinforcement to train behavior is not the same as using mild punishment instead of more severe physical forms. Even mild punishment focuses on correcting mistakes rather

Punishment **has the effect of** *decreasing* **the odds that any behavior it follows will be displayed again sometime in the future.**

Reinforcement **has the effect of** *increasing* **the odds that any behavior it follows will be displayed again sometime in the future.**

than encouraging success. So don't be misled by instructors who call their training approach "positive" when what they really mean is "we aren't as harsh as the others." The only way you can tell what method a trainer truly uses is to watch. Sit in on a class or session before you take your pet. Are the instructors using punishment tools like squirt bottles or prong collars? Do you hear words like alpha, correction, pop, dominate, discipline, or proof, aimed at fixing mistakes? Can you see the trainer forcefully repositioning animals as they heel, sit, stay, or whatever? If you can answer yes to any of these questions, chances are this person is not strictly a reinforcement trainer. So do yourself and your pet a favor and keep searching for another instructor.

In contrast, positive reinforcement training is specific. It communicates *exactly* what behaviors are desired again and again depending, of course, on the skill of the trainer. Animals that are taught what to do in order to gain reinforcement in any circumstance, and who actually get their rewards, will spend more time doing precisely the behaviors they are taught. Logically then, if we fill the animals' day and night with desirable behaviors, they'll have less time and motivation to engage in undesirable behaviors that don't result in reinforcement. This includes the annoying or destructive behaviors we don't want occurring in the first place!

So, you may be thinking, "Why can't I do both? Why can't I use a blend of punishment and reinforcement in training?" Let's see why that won't work. If you are the type of trainer whose focus is about catching animals making mistakes, you won't ever be disappointed—living things make mistakes all the time. But you'll also miss out on the pure joy of just being around your animal, because both of you will always be on guard waiting for the next misstep. That's hardly a trustful situation. By using punishment to train animals, you diminish the quality of the relationship you and your animal may share. It limits the success you'll achieve at home, or in the obedience ring, the vet's office, the stage, or the paddock, whether you are together or apart. Think about it. Punishment shouts, "Stop what you are doing" and "Don't do that again." Reinforcement—the complete opposite—affirms, "Yes, do that again!"

Furthermore, training is not an endpoint but a process. So it's important for trainers to be receptive to the idea of learning from the mistakes animals make, rather than reacting by punishing the behavior. Knowing how, when, and where a behavior breaks down shows us how prepared an animal is for any given situation. It also shows where we should concentrate our future training energy. Trial and error is a part of learning, especially for young animals experiencing the world for the first time. When a wild animal experiments with its surroundings, it may discover new abilities, or develop innovative survival strategies. In training, experimenting can result in new and fun behaviors.

But learning something new at any age depends on a trainee's willingness to take chances and to risk getting it wrong! When trust is built between an animal and caretaker, the result is a confident animal that is willing to follow (or lead) a trainer anywhere, even into new or frightening situations. This trust is built on the certainty that the animal will receive reinforcement not only for successful behaviors, but also for always showing *eagerness to try again, even after a mistake*. It is easy to pick these animals out in a crowd. Even when things don't go as planned, they always return to their trainer with energy, enthusiasm and, if their species has one, with tail wagging.

Conversely, punishment training takes away an animal's desire to try something new out of fear of making mistakes. Over time, punishers shape animals that are timid, aggressive in the face of change, or simply figure out that it is not in their best interest to exert themselves. These animals are easy to spot in a crowd, too. If they return to their trainers, it's done slowly. And if the species happens to have a tail, it's usually tucked between their legs. Using punishment also puts trainers at a disadvantage because it teaches animals to suppress the early warning signs—aggressive behaviors like staring or a low growl—that might otherwise alert caregivers that a serious problem is brewing. For example, ever hear someone say the animal's aggression "came out of nowhere"? How sad and limiting for both the animal and the trainer. The good news is life doesn't have to be that way for either of you.

Reinforcement training opens up so many opportunities to have fun and achieve your goals at the same time. But reinforcement is not a free ride; using it means being proactive and consistent in your behavior expectations. If you want to be successful, you cannot be passive and only react to your pet after it's started an unwanted behavior. You also can't expect your pet to guess what you consider to be appropriate behavior, especially if you're prone to changing the rules from one minute to the next. Training with reinforcement requires you to respond while the animal is displaying desirable behaviors, no matter how it inconveniences you at that moment. It causes you to think ahead and to plan how, when, what, where, and why you intend to "thank" your animal every time it succeeds during the day, not just when it's convenient for you. It also means adjusting your expectations, such as the time involved to teach a new behavior, to match the species, age, skill, and learning history of the animal in question. Reinforcement trainers must be "tuned in" at any given moment or at any stage of development to what the animal needs to be successful.

21

Simply put, if people spent more time reinforcing behaviors they'd like to see repeated, rather than obsessing over commands, criteria, or corrections, they would be amazed by the improvement in their animal's behavior.

Sounds Hard!

You may be thinking this reinforcement stuff seems awfully complex and labor-intensive just to have a household companion. And truthfully, if you're the type of person who focuses only on mistakes and takes all your animal's successes for granted, it may take some practice to adjust your habits. But pet owners beware: you are animal trainers, whether you compete for ribbons or simply want some good company. It is important to remember that animals—yes, even old dogs—are always learning. Thus, we are always training them whether we realize it or not. If you ignore this reality, you'll probably be unhappy with the outcome.

Welcoming an animal into our homes means committing to a lifetime of teaching. Sadly, many pet owners today fail to realize the significance of this commitment, which may be one reason why pet shelters are crowded and why so many unwanted animals are destroyed each year. And since learned behavior is ever changing, pliable, and dynamic, the responsibility for an animal's success lies solely with us, since we are the ones with the expectations. The more *we* expect from an animal, the more *we* are going to have to work at teaching it how to triumph in our world. Happily, with a little effort at the beginning, it gets easier and easier for us to shape constructive behavior and maintain a great relationship with our animal in a way that's healthier for it and more fun for all.

My flying friend, Domingo, and I became living proof that strong training relationships based on mutual trust are possible with positive reinforcement. When he succeeded, I was quick to respond with something fun. If he wandered, I ignored him as best as I could, while ensuring he didn't put himself in harm's way. I never begged for behavior, nor did I ever hold a grudge. Domingo had a few more unscheduled excursions after that first day. However, thanks to zoomility, they became shorter in both distance and time away from home base. Soon, they disappeared altogether as he increasingly sought out my attention. And before I knew it, he'd become our best, most dependable free flight animal—flying to and from stage, not on his schedule, but on ours. I have no doubt this never would have happened if I'd punished him each time he came back to us from one of those early road trips.

For his part, if I had punished him, he surely would not have trusted

22

me enough to reliably return after each requested flight, much less the ones he took on his own. In turn, I would have had my doubts about him as well, and would have chosen instead to rely on other, more dependable birds for flight demonstrations. As a result, his opportunities to experience the most enriching, variable, and successful life possible would have been much more limited. Think about it. How do you *make* a bird fly back to you, especially one that finds you scary, or even boring? It's only through mutual trust that we can hope to advance our relationships beyond merely existing with our animals.

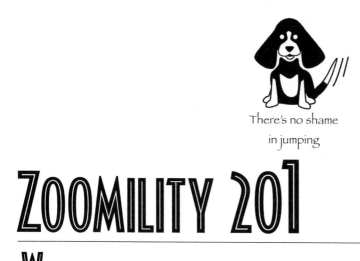

There's no shame
in jumping

ZOOMILITY 201

We've all done dumb things around animals. In my line of work, this seems to happen most often when there's a group of spectators nearby. That's why it's important to learn to laugh at your own mistakes, whether you're the only one who knows, or whether they happen in public view. For one thing, being less self-conscious will make you a better reinforcer. So here's another one of my blunders that stands out in my memory.

One day at the zoo, I was passing by an exhibit when a park guest asked me for help to retrieve her dropped camera. Unfortunately, her camera had fallen over the barrier into the addax paddock. Wanting to provide good customer service and at the same time not wanting the guest to do what I was about to do, I agreed to help. For those who may not have heard of it, the addax is a rather odd-looking antelope. It's mostly white with an almost toupee-like patch of dark brown hair on its head. This gives it a sort of "Moe," of Three Stooges fame, look despite its impressive set of corkscrew-shaped horns. Sadly, this timid hoof-stock species from the harsh Sahara Desert is critically endangered.

The good news for our guests was the recent arrival of a newborn calf in the herd. Good news for the guests—bad news for me! As soon as I hopped the fence to retrieve the camera, I knew I was in trouble. It wasn't like I went anywhere near the youngster, which mom had stashed away in plain view of about a dozen guests. Still, I had misjudged the situation. Apparently, this particular addax was not a comedian. Not only was I not going to have time to pick up the camera, there was serious doubt whether I would make it back over the fence without mom's distinctive horns stuck in my backside. While I have done my best, however unsuccessfully, to avoid it, the truth is there's no shame in getting bit or gored, except on the rump. A trainer's worst fear is a bite on the bottom because everybody knows it means you turned your back and took your eyes off the animal—a classic rookie mistake for sure!

Anyway, my only hope was to treat the fence as a gymnast's pommel horse. Using my left hand as a pivot, I hurled myself horizontally out of the yard in front of all the guests. Shaking off the dust, I checked to see if I'd broken anything important other than my pride. I remember thinking how very stooge-like the experience had been, as I sheepishly radioed for someone to bring me a rake in order to reach down for the camera from the safety of the public side. To this day, the story of the addax remains one of my favorite public "learning opportunities."

In much the same way, it takes courage to change course—to retreat from old punishing or confusing ways of training, even though they may be familiar, comfortable, and easy for us. Changing course means admitting to ourselves that perhaps we, not just our animals, have more to learn, too.

How Do Animals Learn?

Under the heading of "Areas For Improvement," one of my earliest performance evaluations at a zoo listed the phrase "eliminate distractions to training," a favorite expression of my first curator. His goal was to encourage me to take advantage of precious training opportunities by limiting how much time I spent on tasks that did not directly contribute to the animal collection's behavioral repertoire or show quality. But his words could also describe nagging mental distractions.

These "stumbling blocks"[2] include:
- Fip-flopping between the latest training fads or anecdotal methods.
- Anthropomorphism—assigning human thoughts, feelings, and motivations to animals and letting those ideas dictate training decisions rather than the actual behavior of the animal.
- Gaps in our skill and knowledge base.
- Fixating on behavior mistakes instead of behavior successes.

We're all vulnerable to these distractions, particularly when the training program isn't going well and we're wondering why our pet just does not get it. So how do we avoid getting mentally bogged down by dwelling on ideas, experiences, and advice from friends, family, even "experts" whose only effect is to make training matters worse? The answer lies in three simple steps to animal training that I call the 3R's: Request, Response, and Reinforce. The 3R's model is a reinforcement-only version of the more general ABC model of training, which may include reinforcement, punishment or a combination of both.[1, 3]

Using the 3R's model to teach animals will help you eliminate those nagging distractions to training by concentrating your attention only on the aspects of learning that ultimately produce results. Understanding the process by which animals learn will enable you to better guide what your animals do in fact learn. Given this importance, let's explore the 3R's model in more detail.

> **Clues to Cues: The best training cues to teach are ones that are clear, concise, calm, and consistent.**

Requests take many forms and are called by many names such as signals, cues, antecedents, or commands. Regardless of what you choose to call them, most of us are familiar with using auditory, visual, or tactile cues. But even things like tastes and odors can convey important information. In fact, it's staggering to think of the degree to which living things are continuously bombarded by sensory information. How each individual or species organizes, records, recalls, ignores, and/or discards this constant stream of data is a textbook unto itself. The important aspect for trainers to consider is the enormous amount of information an animal processes at any given moment. *We are just one source of sensory information for our animals.* As a result, trainers always need to be aware of the impact outside signals may have on their animal's behavior* and adjust session goals and expectations accordingly. This realization that animals are inundated with a steady stream of information should motivate us to control their learning environment as much as possible. Doing this may reduce the total number of distractions, which will reduce the number of times when our animals choose to ignore us in favor of other cues from the environment.

Response refers to the animal's behavior. For the purpose of this discussion, response means anything the animal does shortly after the request. How soon after the request? The best answer is the sooner, the better. The shorter the time delay between the request and the response, the stronger the association will be between the two.

If this statement is true, why doesn't every piece of incoming sensory

---

* Studies of classical conditioning (e.g., Pavlov's dogs) focused on the role that cues play in eliciting the behaviors that follow them. Operant conditioning examined the impact on learning of stimuli that follow a behavior response. In practice, these distinctions are probably much less important to the typical pet owner, and often, the lines separating these two forms of learning are blurred in real world situations. Given that classical conditioning usually involves simple autonomic responses such as muscle reflexes, the ideas in *Zoomility* were developed with an emphasis on operant conditioning, which encompasses a much larger array of learned behaviors and complex situations. In the end, the most important aspect to remember is that cues communicate information to an animal concerning the appropriateness of engaging in a behavior whether that response is ultimately elicited (classical conditioning) or emitted (operant conditioning). For a more complete discussion of learning through classical and operant conditioning see Chance, 1999, Ramirez, 1999, or Kazdin, 1989.

information result in a behavior response? The answer is that not all possible associations between potential cues and animal behaviors happen. In fact, in most cases there's no connection between incoming stimuli from the environment and the behaviors displayed by the animal at any given moment. That's because there's no immediate consequence to the behavior response—nothing good or bad happens to the animal. So no connection between the request and response is made, and no learning takes place.

Reinforce, the final and most important step in animal training, is a call to action. As we discussed previously, reinforcement is a distinct type of consequence that makes learning possible. When reinforcement immediately follows both the request and the animal's subsequent response, learning takes place. Reinforcing consequences are powerful because they determine whether behaviors are more or less likely to occur again under similar conditions. Plus, they control how tightly animals learn to associate specific requests with the appropriate response. In short, reinforcement is the glue that binds requests and responses together. It drives the learning process and makes animal training possible.

For those who are willing, the 3R's model enables us to harness the learning process to teach the behaviors we want without resorting to punishment. Furthermore, as we'll discover later, the 3R's also help us to prevent the behaviors we don't want our pets to display. Using this model gives any trainer the structure and logic to teach behaviors effectively and efficiently; it also helps create a mindset of cooperation between animal and trainer by *establishing only reinforcing consequences.* The trust and ultimate training success possible with the 3R's far exceeds anything achieved through punishment alone or as a mixture of both punishment and reinforcement. A lot of people, including myself, have bet their lives on it!

Training animals with zoomility is as simple as Request, Response, and Reinforce!

For instance, the first time I was approved to jump in the water with a killer whale for a training session, I wasn't worried about the kind of treatment this animal had received because I knew the 3R's had been used all along. The animal hadn't been raised on punishment, so I did not need to be afraid of how it would behave towards me. For the same reason, I never feared diving from a tower, day after day, holding my breath and blindly waiting for two male bottlenose dolphins to swim from behind to pick me up for the show's dramatic finale. No doubt I would have been a lot less confident about my safety and odds for success if those large animals had been trained with punishment.

Training with the 3R's: Request

Reinforcement trainers should try to think in terms of requesting behavior, not commanding it. This will undoubtedly be a big pill for some to swallow, but it is the essence of what I mean by zoomility. After all, it is unlikely that a trainer, who is at ease with using force or punishment as a consequence would consider their signals as requests. Cues, maybe. Commands most definitely. But requests? No way.

Why is your choice of terminology such a big deal? The answer is, the use of the word *command* implies a level of certainty that anyone who has ever spent a minute training animals knows doesn't exist. Some of my most humbling experiences have been in live audience or television situations where the animal displayed all sorts of behavior other than what was planned or requested. And, while these unscripted responses were usually the source of great entertainment for viewers, they serve as a reminder to all of us that animals, even the most reliable ones, always have choices about whether to engage in a conditioned behavior or not.

Now some readers may argue, quite accurately, that these animals presented on stage or in front of the camera were not properly desensitized, the behaviors in question did not have a sufficient reinforcement history or worse, my reinforcements were simply boring to the animal at that moment. However, the important point is that *commanding* an animal to do certain things at specified times is a misnomer. So why set yourself up for a heaping dose of frustration because you are conditioned to think and feel in terms of the animal defying your commands?

Begin by changing your language, which will inevitably change your outlook.

This statement is important. Feeling a sense of frustration when an animal does something different from what we asked is natural for anyone struggling to meet a training goal, especially if we *feel* like 50 percent of the team isn't holding up its end of the bargain. Using a term like command promises more than can be delivered. It creates a mindset that the trainer is in complete control. So when the animal fails to follow his commands, it's easy for the trainer to feel that he's been wronged. And feeling wronged naturally makes it tempting for us to want to get even. Suddenly, the training session is focused on what the animal has done poorly, rather than what it has done well. Even if we aren't conscious of such thoughts, they can have a profound effect on our actions and on the training relationship we're developing with our pet. When we react out of frustration, training becomes about our ego, not about helping the animal succeed.

What does that mean? It may be something that seems innocuous, like adopting the "we're going to do this until you get it right" strategy. We've all seen it, and maybe even been guilty of it ourselves in the obedience ring, show pool, night house, or horse corral. Sessions that started out aimed at being fun for all involved often degrade into a battle of wills. Or the trainer might behave like a drill sergeant—thinking if one success is good, then doing it many more times in a row must be better. Finally, there are some who respond to animal mistakes with the "one strike and you're out" theory of training, where one mistake means no more positive reinforcement this session.

Since we are all human, these reactions are understandable. But they're also misguided. Remember the earlier example where I mentioned waiting underwater for dolphins to swim by and pick me up? Well, there were shows when I was tempted to think "the boys" were conducting an experiment to see just how long a human can hold his breath underwater. Peering between my legs, with salt water in my eyes, I could just make out their faint shadows several feet behind or below me. I could hear and even feel their echolocation as they scanned me, just out of reach! I was helpless. And then, just when I thought my lungs would burst and I'd have to surface alone to the disappointment of a couple thousand spectators, I'd feel two dolphins under my feet pushing me to the surface. Now, I could have gotten mad and assumed the animals were "playing games" with me, or that "they knew better." But that isn't fair. Furthermore, it's not good science and it's not at all helpful in solving the problem.

Once we examined what was happening, we realized that in our haste to keep the show moving, each of the trainers had gradually accepted slightly longer pick up times, a fraction at a time, which inadvertently reinforced this slow response. Plus, we had become way too predictable about how and when the behavior was reinforced—always at the end of the completed behavior, never at the beginning. Thinking that we were preserving show quality, we rarely took the opportunity to stop and reinforce a quick pick up. Turns out, we were actually weakening the show because the beginning of the behavior slowly degraded. Ultimately, *we*, not the animals were responsible for the decline in the speed of their response, and it was *our* responsibility in the future to reinforce the dolphins for faster criteria at the start of the behavior.

At this point, trainers who are more comfortable with punishment training might be thinking, "This guy's a pushover and a softy. He probably accepts poor criteria. If he's not telling his animals what to do and holding them accountable if they don't follow through, they must be swimming (walking) all over him, figuratively and literally!" I've never understood the belief of traditional punishment trainers who claim that the strict use of positive reinforcement results in lower quality behavior. In actuality, there are countless examples of animals trained solely with positive reinforcement that eagerly engage in conditioned behaviors session after session, show after show, 365 days a year. And yet, when traditional trainers permit themselves to adopt a little zoomility, the ensuing transformation to a life of reinforcement-only training is often astounding and complete. Luckily for me, I landed a training job working with animals and people who opened my eyes.

A similar change of heart happened to a woman who became a long time friend, herself a nationally acclaimed dog obedience trainer, instructor, and breeder. When we first met, she was amazed that reinforced animals at the facility where I was working could accurately display dozens of conditioned behaviors for 15-20 minutes at a time, several performances a day, day after day. In contrast, as a trainer who used to rely on punishment, she encountered countless numbers of dogs conditioned with a heavy hand that couldn't complete more than a couple trials at a weekend obedience competition without shutting down. Once she saw the potential of positive reinforcement, she turned away from using punishment and has encouraged her students and peers to do the same ever since. In light of these examples, it seems clear that positive reinforcement training is by far more likely to condition higher, more consistent criteria.

Before we move on to the next component of learning, a few last words about requests. Requests are valuable, so treat them as such. Think of it this way: every request is an IOU from you to your animal. It conveys a sort of contract offer between the two of you. "If you, the animal, complete my request, I, the trainer, owe you something reinforcing in return." Therefore, don't just toss requests out as if they're meaningless, because meaningless they will become. If you have a habit of repeating the same request one after another (e.g., "Sit, Sit, Sit!"), why should the animal ever bother listening to the first signal? Later, we'll discuss how to offer a request, things to consider before you offer that request, what to do if nothing happens afterward, and most importantly, how to react if something does happen. But for now, your job as a reinforcement trainer is to practice requesting behavior only once and then stop. Observe what happens next and wait! It's the animal's turn to participate in the training process.

Training with the 3R's: Response

The hardest thing to teach a person to do is nothing. Trainers want to "fix" everything immediately.

31

Sometimes, we react too quickly to our animals, even before they've had time to process or problem-solve the request we just made. It's as if we want to will them to learn by doing it for them. Tempting as it may be, thinking on behalf of our animals is not all that helpful. It simply does not prepare them to meet the day's challenges when we aren't around. *For a trainer, learning to remain calm, motionless, and silent, and to suppress knee-jerk reactions immediately after requesting a behavior is one of the most valuable skills that can be learned.* Not only is it useful when the animal responds correctly, but as we'll discuss later, it's also extremely helpful when the animal responds incorrectly!

How does it work? Get into the habit of offering a request and waiting for your animal's response. As you wait, note everything that occurs over the next few seconds. The most successful trainers I've ever encountered are the ones with an eye for detail. Being able to stay still and note subtle changes in behavior can lead to greater training accomplishments. Luckily, anyone can learn to be more observant. It just takes practice and a clear idea of exactly what *you* want the outcome to be. Having a clear mental picture of what you ultimately want the behavior to be serves as a benchmark, allowing you to compare what the actual behavior is today with your goal. You simply can't get to your destination if you don't know where you want to go.

Since training progress is usually made in small steps, we begin by breaking down complex behaviors into smaller parts, called approximations. Some trainers call a series of approximations a behavior *pyramid, ladder,* or *flow chart.* Whatever visual you prefer to use, the process is like a cooking recipe. Before you start, you need to determine what ingredients are required, what steps need to be followed to produce the desired response, and what the finished product should look like.

An *approximation* is a simple behavior that resembles some part of the final behavior. For example, bending the legs is an approximation of sitting.

Despite occasional similarities, chances are your behavior recipes will look very different from mine or anyone else's. It's easy to see why. The different paths leading to a desired behavior are as variable as the number of creative people thinking of ways to get there.[4] That's part of the art of training, the part that allows us to put our own inventive stamp on each behavior. Some training experts will have you believe there's only one strict set of instructions to follow in order to teach a given behavior such as heeling. These folks insist you must follow their recipe word for word and step by step for all animals. In contrast, just like in cooking, I let the ingredients I have on hand, such as the knowledge and behav-

for most situations—unless you're teaching musical chairs.

The secret to quickly and efficiently teaching a behavior is to help animals understand what components you expect of them by keeping the training instructions simple! How? First, identify the components of complex behaviors and break them down into approximations or simple steps your animal can understand using these four quantifiable elements. Second, communicate them to the animal.

So before you get near your student and start your next training session, think about the behavior you want your animal to learn. Imagine what approximations you want to teach your pet in terms of duration, energy, frequency, and topography. Then, design training sessions that incorporate each of the 4 components. Let's walk through the sit example to really bring this to life. Initially, you'll want to work on only one or two of the four components at a time. For example, you might concentrate on improving the animal's ability to remain sitting for longer duration when you can conduct a session in a comfortable, familiar, less distracting setting, like your home. However, if you take your animal to a new, exciting, distracting, or potentially scary location, you might want to lower your duration expectations (don't expect him to sit as long) in favor of reinforcing success in a more complex environment (getting him to sit at all when there's so much excitement to distract him). In other words, during the initial training process, as you ask for more criteria in one aspect of the behavior such as topography, or the new location, you need to be prepared to relax your criteria in other areas such as duration.[4] Eventually, as the animal gets better at each component, you'll be able to raise the criteria on all components together to form one complex finished behavior. Stay tuned for much more on this once we discuss the last of the 3R's, reinforce, which is by far the most important ingredient to learning.

If your head is beginning to spin keeping track of requests, responses, approximations, and criteria measured in terms of duration, energy, frequency, and topography, you're not alone! This is a lot of information to track for one animal, let alone a zoo or house full of creatures. This is exactly why the most successful keepers record their observations about their animals every day. The best advice I can offer is to write things down and to reread your notes before planning the next session. A gifted friend of mine spends several minutes cataloging her training sessions on a daily basis. Sometimes her notes are brief, other times she writes pages about what worked and what didn't. Most importantly, I've seen her study her notes before working through the next set of challenging approximations. As a result, she is a far better trainer today because she took the time to record her ups and downs and those of the creatures under her care. You can bet her animals have benefited from it, too.

Training with the 3R's: Reinforce

In the previous section, I stated that the art of training is reflected in the diverse ways in which trainers approximate behaviors using their own unique behavior recipes. Some recipes may be more efficient than others. All that really matters is that the *desired* behavior is learned. Ultimately, the set of behavior approximations you choose will be unique to you, your animal, and the environment in which you work. The part of training that should not be different from trainer to trainer is how we react to successful approximations—with reinforcement, not punishment. Now let's talk about what actually counts as reinforcement.

Positive reinforcement can be anything. As with approximation recipes, the list of what can become positive reinforcement to an animal is limited only by the creativity of the trainer. Unlike punishment, whose escalating forms have a natural limit called death, there is almost no limit to the number of things that can be reinforcing. Just to be clear, the positive in *positive reinforcement* refers to something that is *applied* to the animal such as giving it a ball or a back scratch. Conversely, *negative reinforcement* is anything *removed* from the animal or its surroundings that has a reinforcing effect on behavior, such as removing something the animal is afraid of. Later, we'll talk a bit more about negative reinforcement and how it can often occur in an animal's environment beyond our control. We'll also discuss the downside of using negative reinforcement.

First, the positive. By definition, reinforced behaviors are more likely to occur again in the future. But how do we know what is positive reinforcement? That's easy. Let the animal's response or behavior be your guide. For instance, does the animal appear to like the item you just offered? Does it take the toy from you, or does it run away in fear? To determine whether something has positive reinforcement value to an animal, we must take note of its responses to what we offer. For example, does that new squeak toy really have reinforcing qualities or does it annoy your pet as much as it does the neighbors? Think back to how we measure the criteria of a behavior response using the DEFT categories: does the desired behavior occur for longer duration, with greater energy, more frequently, or in a new context following delivery of the squeak toy? If the behavior in question is more consistent, or more likely to occur again, the toy is a reinforcer. If the behavior is not improved, the "reward" is not a good choice.

Usually, figuring out what is reinforcing to an animal isn't all that complicated. But it is important to remember that *the animal's idea of reinforcement may not be the same as yours.* Keeping this in mind may save you hundreds of dollars in pet toys at the checkout counter. If you want to learn what is reinforcing to your animals, try spying on them. Spying is useful for many reasons. Observing them as they find their own reinforcement can help enhance your creativity and may even give you ideas for new behaviors to train. I recall my first season at a marine animal park watching the area supervisor spend much of his down time studying the animals, observing them during their own playtimes, and occasionally interacting with them in unusual places throughout their habitat.

Training tip: Try spying on your animals to find out how they spend their time and what reinforcements they prefer the most.

All this effort after he did so many exhausting shows! I've always admired the commitment he demonstrated, especially when all I wanted to do was "take five" and catch my breath. When I finally asked him why he wasn't using the time to rest before the next show, he replied that he was studying what made that individual animal tick. His point was that our job was not merely to apply any old reinforcement that we find convenient, but to apply the best, most desirable reinforcement available to match the animal's need at any given moment. The better we are at anticipating their ever-changing reinforcement needs, the stronger our learning sessions will be.

As you've probably guessed, timely application of positive reinforcement is central to animal learning. It is by far the most important component of training with the 3R's. Yet we've only scratched the surface when it comes to understanding all of its facets. In the next chapter we'll examine reinforcement and its potential in a bit more detail.

When one door
opens

ZOOMILITY 301

Keepers open and close thousands of gates over the course of a zoo career. While every latched gate is important, there are some you absolutely don't want to forget to close. A mistake can mean lives are at risk. Speaking on this subject, a friend of mine who works with elephants shared this zoomility story with me.

"I'm embarrassed to say that we accidentally left a gate open one time, allowing an elephant access to a keeper area. This meant she was outside the perimeter of her exhibit and easily could have broken through an adjacent, human gate into the general public area. Obviously, this was potentially a very scary situation for all of us because the elephant was someplace unfamiliar to her.

The thing that saved us was the fact that we had strong relationships with the elephants. No punishment was ever used. You see, from the moment this group had arrived at our park, we began positively reinforcing each one for focusing its attention on the trainer. This enabled us to begin teaching all sorts of cooperative behaviors including one called an A to B behavior—the animal voluntarily moves on request from one trainer's location to another somewhere inside its exhibit. So, as time passed and the elephants became more trusting of us, we were able to systematically ask the elephants to move through the many elephant gates to different yards and barns.

So when the gate was left open, by remaining clear and calm with the elephant, we were safely able to open up another gated section and ask her back onto her exhibit like it was a normal A to B behavior.

Thanks to a little quick thinking and relationships based on trust, she and the other elephants allowed us to make some unusual changes to keep all humans and animals out of harm's way."

Wow. When it comes to successfully training with zoomility, the size of the challenge or the species really doesn't matter.

Reinforcement Unleashed

At the heart of zoomility is learning to use the 3R's to train animal behavior. As we discovered in the last chapter, the glue that holds our requests and the animal's subsequent responses together is positive reinforcement. Simply put, reinforcement increases the likelihood that the preceding responses will be repeated the next time we make the request. Still, some obvious questions about reinforcement remain. Are all reinforcements created equal? If something is reinforcing today, will it always be reinforcing in the future? Can something that is neutral or, worse, scary to an animal today ever become reinforcing in the future?

To answer, we only need to look at our own likes and dislikes. Everyday experience tells us that not all reinforcements have the same impact. Some reinforcements are intrinsic to an animal's survival, which means the animal does not need to learn to like them. Food, air, water, and sex are examples of naturally occurring reinforcers that don't need to be taught. Scientists call them primary reinforcers, not because they come first, but because they are essential for life.

Other things may become reinforcers through experience. For example, money is just paper, plastic, or metal. You can't survive by eating it; yet we learn to associate money not only with primary reinforcers that enable us to survive, but also with many other things that make living pleasant. Money by itself is not absolutely essential for life. However, it does provide things that make living easier and more interesting. Thus, money is a *conditioned reinforcement* (also referred to as a secondary reinforcement). For instance, the desire for money increases the likelihood that people go to work every week to earn a paycheck, allowing them to buy the things necessary for survival.

Conditioned reinforcements such as the value of money are learned, as opposed to primary reinforcements that are intrinsic to an animal. Conditioned reinforcers gain strength by being associated or paired with other reinforcements. As a result, the world is filled with all sorts of objects and activities that can become potential conditioned reinforcements if we just learn how to teach them to our pet. This is a powerful training concept. It not only unlocks the secret to maintaining animal behavior with positive reinforcement, but it also forms the basis for counter-conditioning fears and phobias as well as teaching some complex, and even uncomfortable veterinary behaviors like nail clipping or voluntary blood sampling.

How does this work? Remember, conditioned reinforcers are learned. So anything can be taught to become reinforcing. With care, even previously scary things or situations can become conditioned reinforcers. This means trainers don't have to restrict their reinforcements to just a small set of things the animal naturally finds rewarding, such as food. Just imagine the behavior training possibilities if your animal learns the whole world is its toy chest and you hold the key!

So which reinforcers are best to use? Well, you don't have to be a reinforcement-only trainer to know that food is one of the most potent and easy to use reinforcers. But food also has its limitations. Eventually animals do fill up. Plus, that last bite of kibble probably doesn't have the same impact on learning as the first, when the animal was hungrier. Clearly, unraveling the mysteries of the brain's biochemical response to all types of reinforcement is beyond the scope of this book. Though at least one conclusion is clear: the reinforcement values of things, even food, can and do change, particularly as animals become satiated. Familiar toys grow tiresome after long use. Left unchanged, backyards, kennels, or exhibits can get rather dull day after day. Overfed or sick animals may refuse to eat more treats. Even activities, which themselves can be reinforcing, can lose value, if requested over and over again. So when you're selecting a reinforcer for your animal, remember the old saying about absence, because it truly does make the heart grow fonder. As a general rule, the best, most effective reinforcements are often the ones the animal hasn't experienced in a while. In the end, it's not as important to know the difference between primary and conditioned reinforcements, as it is to know and offer whatever is most rewarding to your animal at any given moment.

Build a Bridge...and Use It

There is one more concept related to reinforcement called a *bridge* that deserves special attention. In training jargon, a bridge is a unique, conditioned reinforcer that is used to let the animal know it has successfully completed a behavior. The expression was coined when some of the pioneers in marine mammal training used a whistle as acknowledgement for completing successful approximations when the animals were far from the trainer, such as in a midair jump. Their purpose was to teach the animals to accept a time delay between completing the behavior (i.e., reaching the highest point of the jump) and swimming back to the trainer to actually receive some reinforcement. The whistle served as a conditioned reinforcer to "bridge" the gap of time and distance between completing the behavior and obtaining meaningful reinforcement.

A bridge may take many forms, including a sound like a whistle, a spoken word, or a clicker. It can also be other sensations like a touch,

A bridge is not a permanent substitute for giving a more meaningful form of reinforcement.

a double tap on the body, a point of the trainer's finger, a wink, and so on. An obedience trainer friend once used pushing up her glasses on her nose as a bridge! Like any reinforcement, a bridge can be anything that's practical for you, your animal, and your situation. In fact, it's sometimes all too easy to condition a bridge or two without realizing it. For example, a friend of mine uses an electric can opener every time she feeds her cats. The cats have learned to associate the sounds of the cupboard opening, the can tapping on the counter top, and especially the distinct noise of the opener with a tasty meal that often follows these events. Now, even if she simply turns on the opener, the cats come calling. If she were to switch to feeding her animals dry food, the opener would eventually lose its reinforcing value since the connection between the sound and the primary reinforcement of canned food would be gone.

To maintain the strength and effectiveness of the bridge, trainers must continually associate it with other reinforcers such as praise, food items, toys, or tactile reinforcement. It's also important to maintain the consistency of the bridge, whatever it may be. For example, if you use a calm "Good" or "Ok" as a signal, it shouldn't change to "GOOD!" or "OK, OK, OK!" just because you are excited or agitated. This may be one of the reasons clickers have been so popular lately. In addition to being based on the use of positive reinforcement, they offer the advantage of producing a consistent sound each and every time. So if you need the consistency of a whistle or clicker, get one. But don't think it's essential. A calmly spoken word or soft touch will do just as well. Besides, if you lose your clicker, does that mean you can't reward your animal? Of course not! Anything can be conditioned to be a bridge as long as you maintain it with significant reinforcement. Find what works best for your situation.

Now here's a word of caution about the bridge. As with all conditioned reinforcers, the bridge is only as good as the last time it was reinforced by something meaningful to the animal. If you toot, click, or shout "Good boy!" all day long without taking time to *frequently* stop and add other forms of reinforcement to your training, your animal will lose interest. By itself, the bridge simply becomes noise animals will eventually learn to forget or ignore.

To illustrate, I remember being a bit confused during my first summer training dolphins while watching the area supervisor feed out leftover show food collected from various reinforcement stations strategically placed around the stage. Several

To maintain its effectiveness, use a bridge sparingly and follow it with other reinforcements as much as possible.

minutes at a time I'd hear "toot" followed by a few fish tossed into their mouths—primary reinforcement *I thought* would be better spent teaching a new behavior. Then another "toot," fish, "toot," more fish, and so on until the bucket was empty. What I came to understand was that despite working with dolphins that had heard the same whistle bridge thousands of times over many years, *he was actively reinforcing the bridge.* By doing so, he replenished the value of the "toot" even with animals that had heard that sound most of their lives. All the dolphins had to do was sit up and remain attentive!

As he explained to me, it's like putting money into a savings account. Every time we bridge a response and quickly move on to the next behavior request without stopping to add significant reinforcement, we weaken the impact of the bridge. We may find ourselves doing this when we are trying to build an animal's motivation, adding to the show's quality, following obedience competition rules which prohibit offering reinforcement in the ring, or simply when we don't have any other reinforcements available. As a result of neglecting the bridge by not backing it up with meaningful reinforcers, learning will degrade in time. It's like taking money out and never putting money back into the account. Eventually, the account will be empty and worthless.

As you can see, reinforcement is really the key to all animal training, and without a doubt, the most important component of the 3R's. Moreover, because reinforcement is so important, it is necessary to explore a few related topics before we put the 3R's all together with an animal in front of us to actually train a behavior.

Desensitization: Reinforcing Animals to Ignore Any Distraction Without Fear

Before you try to teach something to be reinforcing, it's a good idea to make sure your animal isn't deathly afraid of whatever it is. This process is called *desensitization.* Using it, we can actively help animals become accustomed to new sensations through sight, sound, smell, taste, and touch that come in the form of other people, things, places, activities, or animals.

Desensitization is the deliberate application of positive reinforcement as a consequence for calm responses to new or frightening things, sensations, or events.

Desensitization training is so important to achieving your ultimate behavioral goals that every behavior recipe you develop should begin with an assessment of the animal's current level of desensitization and what additional work, if any, is needed. For example, it's probably not going to be easy to teach a "sit" if the animal is afraid of the slippery, waxed floor where you're both standing. In the same way, there isn't much sense in trying to approximate an ultrasound exam on a dolphin's body if each time you turn on the vibrating probe the animal's acute hearing causes it to break from position and swim away. It's even possible that some animals may need to be desensitized to objects we think are reinforcing, such as pet toys!

Sometimes trainers simply place new objects in an animal's habitat and expect them to "work it out." This process is called *habituation.* While it is true that animals can and do learn to accept things in their environment through this passive process, it's also true that complete habituation can take forever. Furthermore, it's possible that animals left on their own may become more, rather than less afraid of new objects in their environment.

For instance, imagine you purchase a new dog crate to contain your dog while you're not at home. This can be a useful solution provided you take the time to desensitize the animal to being inside the crate for extended periods of time. However suppose, on the first day, you're running late and decide to simply "place" the animal inside and leave for work. When you come home, you find a panting and somewhat frantic animal that has spent the past few hours chewing a hole in your new kennel. Feeling a bit guilty, you open the door, letting the agitated animal bolt out. The next day, you try to get the animal to enter the crate on its own accord, with zero success. Being there yesterday was no fun—why would it want to go in again today? So you again resort, this time forcefully, to placing the animal inside. This time it immediately begins pacing and scratching at the door. Instead of being desensitized (getting used to the crate), the animal is *firmly sensitized to the new enclosure,* having learned the first day to be afraid of being trapped in it.

It's far better to actively train animals through a deliberate desensitization plan to help them learn that new things are no big deal, rather than leaving it up to chance and assuming they'll figure it out on their own. Why? Because, there's always a chance that the behavior you intended to teach could go in the other direction, making matters worse. Animals that aren't desensitized often learn the opposite of what we intend. In this example, placing the dog in the crate for short times during feeding could have helped it learn to tolerate being in the kennel. Leaving it alone for long periods before it learned to feel safe in the kennel helped the dog learn to be afraid.

Part of the reason for this is a phenomenon we've briefly mentioned before, called *negative reinforcement.* The easiest way to comprehend the meaning of negative reinforcement is to think of the word "escape." Negative reinforcement occurs when things animals perceive as aversive or punishing are removed from the immediate environment. For example, let's say a zoo veterinarian wears a bright red jacket at each weekly visit. This visit can be a frightening event, especially for wild, untrained animals that may require medical attention. After just the first visit, these animals may learn to associate a red coat with being frightened or experiencing minor discomfort from something like a routine injection. In the future, they may run away, or escape at the first sign of any person wearing a bright red jacket.

In this case, the response of running away (escaping) is negatively reinforced. The animal engages in behaviors that enable it to avoid the person in the red jacket because it perceives the person to be the source of discomfort. When the animal runs away, it doesn't receive a shot. This result makes the probability of future escape behaviors more likely because the perceived aversive (the shot), associated with a person in a red jacket, is removed from the environment. In this example, the animal's own actions caused the apparent removal of this unpleasant event. Thus, one big problem with negative reinforcement is that it usually encourages fearful, escape-like behaviors, rather than relaxed, cooperative ones. Of course, the other problem is it depends on the removal of a punishing consequence. This means there had to be a punishment there in the first place.

Let's refer back to the previous example of introducing a new dog crate. By rushing through without taking time to desensitize the animal to the new object, the trainer actually created an aversive event when he placed the animal inside the unknown enclosure and left it there. We can conclude this based on the destruction of the kennel and the animal's escape (i.e., negative reinforcement) once the door was opened. Through its own actions, the animal was able to remove the perceived punishment of being inside the crate. The next day, not only is there likely to be more punishment associated with the enclosure due to the previous day's experience, but the animal has also been negatively reinforced for fleeing the crate, not for entering it. In other words, not only does the animal want to avoid the kennel, it was reinforced for running away from it—a double whammy.

If you're still fuzzy on negative reinforcement, here's another example. Suppose you are considering enclosing your pet with an electric fence such as a hotwire or shock collar. These systems are based on the inescapable bond between punishment and negative reinforcement. Animals can make the shock, punishment they receive for approaching an electric fence line, stop by backing away from it. The behavior that immediately precedes the end of the punishment or removal of the shock is avoiding the fence. By terminating the shock, the act of moving away from the fence perimeter is negatively reinforced and will more likely occur in the future. Sadly, many other punishment training devices and techniques exist on the market that rely on this same principle of removing pain, or the threat of pain, to negatively reinforce behaviors. Some examples are prong collars, choke collars, the ear pinch, and electric shock training mats and collars. At their core, these gadgets depend on applying (or the threat of applying) some form of punishment first, which when removed, negatively reinforces behavior.

The inevitable link between punishment and negative reinforcement underscores the importance of desensitization training to prevent unwanted learning. For those who do not purposefully punish animals, the obvious lesson is to realize that the world is still filled with things or events that are potentially scary or painful to animals. Sometimes, these potentially punishing events are under our control, such as the appearance of a new crate. Often they are not. Whether these controllable or uncontrollable events become a signal for the animal to flee or to remain calm depends on us. The key is to be aware of the possible negative reinforcement that may occur when animals escape from these punishers.

If we're fortunate, we'll have anticipated and prepared for any possible unpleasant event before it occurs so we can avoid it. At the very least, we should try to react in a way that helps desensitize the animal to similar situations in the future. Of course, sometimes we may be just as surprised by circumstances as the animal. In either case, our job as trainers is to make matters better, not worse. As we describe in greater detail in the upcoming recipe section, here's how we do this:

- Never deliberately punish animals.
- Actively work to desensitize animals (through approximations) to new events, objects, activities, and so on.
- Prevent any accidental positive or additional negative reinforcement if fearful responses do occur.
- Positively reinforce, when possible, a calm response that is incompatible with an escape response.

Following these steps may mean the difference between an animal that is fearful of new things and new situations, and one that is confident and responds calmly in the face of sudden changes in its environment.

Variable Reinforcement

Even reinforcement has its limits. For example, if you always use the same items or actions to reward your animals, they'll eventually become bored. They may even try to find their own reinforcement in ways you won't appreciate, such as digging up your garden, chewing your leather couch, barking at the neighbor's kids, or getting into the trash, just to name a few. Furthermore, there may be times when you want to increase an animal's motivation in order to raise

> **Change itself can be reinforcing, especially for animals taught with zoomility. Alternate the reinforcers you use and try varying the location and order in which behaviors are requested.**

behavior criteria. To do this, it's important to vary the types and amounts of reinforcers you use in training sessions. Nothing says "tummy's full, time for a nap" more than a package of hotdogs fed out in the first few minutes of a session!

Unfortunately, trainers, who make the initial switch from training with punishment to training with reinforcement, sometimes fall into the habit of reinforcing everything in the same manner. It is easy to understand why. In many cases, these trainers, who often reinforce with food treats, are so pleased by the improvements in their pet's behavior that they never advance to the next level. This is not to say that food used as a reinforcer is a bad thing. On the contrary, it's better for new trainers to use food reinforcements for everything rather than revert to using punishment. But a common criticism of reinforcement training by traditional trainers is that it depends solely on food. This isn't true. But it may appear that way when some of us fall into the habit of only giving treats because they work so well. This is especially true when animals and trainers are coming from a history where punishment was the norm. So use food reinforcements all you want, but don't stop there. The world can be much more interesting for your animal when you use a variety of reinforcements, including favorite food items from time to time. Plus, you'll be able to raise behavior criteria to greater heights by varying the reinforcements you offer.

> **Sadly, many animals unaccustomed to learning in a reinforcement-only setting have a difficult time adjusting to even small changes made to their environment, behavior sequences, or reinforcements. *Change* often leads them to respond with frustration and aggression.**

In fact, one of the best ways to use food is as reinforcement to other possible reinforcers such as toys, activities, new social companions, a bridge, and so on. For example, some animals respond well to being groomed while others do not. One way to make grooming fun for the tactile-challenged animal is to reinforce her with food items immediately after she sits calmly during a little brushing. Assuming your animal is desensitized to the mere presence of the brush or comb in your hand, you can follow every light pass over her body with a favorite treat. You'll

> **Every behavior response you hope will be repeated again in the future can and should be reinforced, each time.**

quickly shape an animal that willingly lines up for grooming each and every time. Eventually, being brushed will be fun in itself, without the need for food each time.

At this point, an obvious question might be whether every behavior response can and should be reinforced. The answer is yes. Doing so "shows them the difference" between success and failure. Perhaps the more important question is, should all those reinforcements be the same type, be of equal value, or have the same impact? The answer, which may surprise you, is no. The power of reinforcement to produce desirable behaviors comes from its variability of form, size, and timing. Not only is it important to vary the types, it's critical to vary the timing and magnitude of reinforcements in order to keep them unpredictable. The reason? *When animals can predict the outcome of a training session by knowing when, where, and what reinforcement is coming, they can and often do assume greater control of that session.* This is a particularly troublesome situation for the trainer if the reinforcement they planned to use is already recognized by the animal and is something the animal isn't all that excited about. Predictability of reinforcement leads to boredom, which often leads to unwanted outcomes.

For example, suppose you're trying to teach your dog to jump over a bar. Because this response requires some exertion, you're looking to reinforce approximations that reflect more intensity than, say, a sit behavior. There are several approximations leading up to a successful jump, which include but are not limited to patiently sitting beside the trainer, making good eye contact in order to receive the request to jump, a quick take off following the request, running fast and straight for the bar, and so on. But what

> **A good supply of conditioned reinforcers enables us to teach *and maintain* all those little behaviors that we may otherwise take for granted, such as making eye contact with us and being ready for the next request.**

if you feed every one of these approximations leading up to a successful jump in the same training session? How likely are you to get the maximum amount of effort from your animal at the point of actually jumping over the bar after giving it several successive food items in a row? The answer is, not very—especially, since many of those approximations leading up to a high energy jump are actually low energy behaviors such as "sit there and look at the trainer" for the next request.

Once it is applied, reinforcement satisfies a portion of the animal's needs at that instant. Depending on the size and type of reinforcers you use, the animal may become quite satiated, and therefore show much less motivation for the next behavior request, especially if that next request requires some exertion! Think about your own motivation to do anything but sleep or *watch* football after eating a big dinner on Thanksgiving Day. The solution to avoid satiating your animals quickly, especially with food, is to have a large arsenal of conditioned reinforcers, including a strong bridge, available to you and your animals.

A similar trap some trainers fall into is overuse of the *jackpot* approach to reinforcement. These jackpots or *magnitude reinforcers*, such as huge handfuls of treats, are delivered with the intent to show animals just how much we like a certain response, sometimes to the exclusion of all other good responses. If you use jackpots too often, your animals will quickly be satiated and their motivation may plunge. If you use them sparsely, you risk frustrating or boring your animals due to a lack of reinforcement. There's no doubt that surprising your animals for a job well done with a large amount of reinforcement such as food can be very effective. Still, it's important to vary the size of our reinforcements to avoid becoming predictable to our pets. As with all reinforcement opportunities, the answer is to be variable in how and when a jackpot is applied. Give jackpots for behaviors that require exertion, but occasionally change it. Be creative and give large reinforcements for the everyday, low energy, but high criteria responses once in a while, too.

It's also a good idea to match reinforcers to the behavior you are trying to teach, again, without becoming predictable or boring. In other words, some behaviors require minimal effort and might be better suited to low energy reinforcements. Other behaviors demand extra effort and may benefit from energetic reinforcers. For example, no matter the species, drawing blood voluntarily requires calm, relaxed animals that must often remain motionless for several minutes at a time. Furthermore, in the case of dolphins, they also have to hold their breath! So it may actually be counterproductive to the desired behavior if the animal is excited or tense in anticipation of its favorite boomer ball splashing near its head, or a companion animal barreling into the area for playtime. That's not to say that these aren't good reinforcers, at the appropriate time. But when such calm and precise responses are needed, you might want to initially provide a calm reinforcer and then move on to something with a little more energy later. For instance, you can use a relaxing body massage to help shape a calm blood draw, body exam, nail clipping, etc. Then a few minutes later, as part of a significant reinforcement for a job well done, you can introduce a favorite tennis ball, food treat, or some other lively reinforcers.

Conversely, when reacting to high intensity behaviors, like those involved in completing an agility course, you might start with robust reinforcers such as clapping, jumping up and down, tossing a ball or treat, etc. Then shift into something calmer like a long, slow back scratch. This will allow your animal to differentiate between situations that require high and those that require low energy.

Great trainers choose reinforcers that help shape the next approximation.

Variable Placement of Reinforcement

There are so many more aspects to reinforcement that we could discuss, but one of the most important is the actual placement of reinforcement. As a matter of practicality, trainers often reinforce animals when they are in close proximity. This makes sense because most behaviors begin and end with an animal next to the trainer. But sometimes behaviors require animals to leave our side without the aid of a leash, such as a "go-out" in obedience training in which a dog is asked to leave the trainer, move to a distant location, and then remain at that station. In this situation, it's usually not practical or helpful in shaping the go-out behavior to reinforce the animal next to the trainer. Let me explain.

To begin, think of reinforcement as a magnet and the animal as a piece of steel. In general, the more reinforcement we apply at a certain location or specific topography, the stronger the attraction of the animal towards the source of that reinforcement. Since most of us *are* (or hope to be) the source of reinforcement for our animals, this is a great feature if we *always* want our animals at our side. But sometimes we want our animals to be able to respond well away from us, such as in the case of the go-out behavior. Here, reinforcing the dog next to us would be counterproductive. Look at it from the animal's perspective. "If I always get reinforced next to you, why would I eagerly leave your side?" In this example, the trainer's technique is confusing—it communicates "go away from me, but expect reinforcement for staying by me."

In theory, the criteria of a go-out behavior requires the animal to continue away from the trainer along a straight path until given further information such as to stop, change direction, stay, or turn around and sit. In practice, predictability in the form of the size of the obedience ring often communicates when and where the dog should stop, not the trainer. The criteria for the behavior is not to inch slowly away and stop at some nearby distance of the dog's own choosing. Unfortunately, this is often what happens as a result of predictable approximations that are always reinforced when the animal is in close proximity.

To begin teaching a "leave my side," "fly from me," or any distal off lead behavior, place most of the reinforcement away from you.

Even trainers who use a bridge when the animal is far away can run into problems if they *always* back up their bridge with a toy or food reinforcer *upon the animal's return*. Why? A whistle or clicker bridge, while useful, is not a permanent substitute for an actual toy, treat, or pat on the head. Ask yourself, which you would rather have? A familiar, often overused sound that is far away, or a scratch behind the ears by your best friend? Founding Father, Ben Franklin, could have been speaking about animal training with the famous quip that "actions" really do "speak louder than words."

The solution is to preplan when and where you intend to reinforce in order to shape the behavior you are trying to teach. Before training any behavior, know ahead of time where you want the animal to end up (e.g., near or far away) and what you want it to be doing (e.g., low or high energy response). That's also where you'll want to concentrate a large portion of the reinforcement for that behavior approximation. Be careful! If you always reinforce your animals away from you, the opposite problem will occur—they won't come back. The key is to have a balanced approach to reinforcement. Start by tossing reinforcement *past* the animal or have someone else at a distance provide it. Or, if you don't have a human helper to assist you, you can at least take animals to distant locations where you have secretly hidden reinforcers before the session began. In later sessions, as the animal begins to understand the concept that it will still be reinforced for being away from you, shift the balance back to you just a bit. That way you'll quickly teach a straight and long go-out, retrieve, free flight, etc. and your animal will still be motivated to come back.

> **Trainers who provide positive and variable reinforcements don't have to worry about animals that wander in search of their own reinforcement or seek to escape punishment.**

Did you notice I suggested tossing the reinforcement past the animal, not to him or in front of him, once he's turned around to face you? Why? Tossing it past the animal helps teach that in order to gain reinforcement, the animal must "go away." If you toss it directly to him (or anywhere between the two of you), you may end up teaching the opposite concept by making him turn back toward you to get the reinforcer. Think about which direction the animal is facing when the reinforcement arrives. It's more consistent with shaping a go-out to give reinforcement while the animal is facing away from you. In any session, avoid this common training paradox: my intentions (i.e., requests) communicate one thing but my reactions (i.e., reinforcements) communicate another. Trainers should always keep in mind whether the reinforcement they are applying at any moment actually helps to encourage the concept they are trying to teach or undercuts it.

If you think about it, behaviors like the go-out present punishment trainers with a dilemma. Such trainers may be inclined to recall their animal in order to punish an incorrect behavior approximation. If the animal is leashed, the trainer might jerk the lead in order to pop them back into position to deliver the correction. But what if the animal is off lead? Here, the animal must voluntarily "come" to receive a punishment. Now seriously, how quickly would you return knowing you were about to get punished?

Placing reinforcement in the right location at the right time helps to shape behavior. Learning where and when to apply appropriate reinforcement will help you clearly communicate your behavior expectations. If animals are hesitant to leave your side, place future reinforcement away from you. If animals take too long to return to you, shift the source of reinforcement back to you. Such regular adjustment of reinforcement placement will enable you to shape behaviors that result in better criteria in far less time.

In conclusion, *the maximum power of positive reinforcement training comes when the animal has absolutely no idea when, where, or what type of reinforcer is coming next.* By using desensitization and variable reinforcers, you will teach animals that unpredictable change is a good thing. And *that* is one of the most powerful reinforcers of all.

Relationship to
the rescue

ZOOMILITY 401

Nothing can match the power of positive reinforcement in building a relationship of trust between humans and animals. Yet animals, like people, are not perfect. Mistakes happen and low criteria are sometimes a part of life. So how can we remain true to our goal of only using reinforcement to shape superior behaviors without using punishment when mistakes do happen? Reinforcement training is so much more than simply bribing animals with food, and it definitely is not about accepting mediocre behavior criteria as some critics contend. To illustrate, here's another true story that still leaves a knot in my stomach.

Despite enormous job satisfaction, working in a zoo facility is hard—there's always something to clean. Even animal pools filled with filtered water require regular scrubbing. This usually involved scuba diving one empty pool at a time with one of those floppy vacuum heads and miles of hose behind you. For larger debris, it was sometimes necessary to remove the vacuum head and use just the hose.

It happened that a coworker and I spent an afternoon vacuuming the killer whale pools. When we were done, we fed out the day's fish and gave the whales access to all the pools. That's when I noticed that the vacuum head was missing from its usual storage bucket. Instantly, my friend and I turned pale as images flashed through our minds of a plastic vacuum head in the belly of an irreplaceable animal. Apparently, we had forgotten it at the bottom of one of the pools.

Immediately, he ran to the whales and began a training session as I scoured the poolside looking for the missing part. He had no bucket of fish to feed... no time to grab a pile of toys for the whales to play with... only his relationship with the animals to hold their attention. I finally located the vacuum head in about 10 feet of water. I grabbed a pole and started fishing for the missing part. Our curious whales were intrigued by the unusual activity and clamoring sounds I was making nearby. They certainly could have broken station at any time to investigate what I was doing. But they didn't, and I was able to slowly work the vacuum head out of the water. Armed only with his relationship with the animals based on positive reinforcement, my friend was able to hold their attention and keep them safe as I scrambled to retrieve the part and avert a potential disaster.

I imagine our zoo careers might have been a lot shorter if those animals hadn't been trained with positive reinforcement of all kinds, if they hadn't been actively desensitized to changes in their habitat, and if these giant predators were motivated solely by food. If my friend and I could depend on the 3R's to save the day, surely we can use them to teach animals to survive the "wild" in our own homes.

You're Ready to Reinforce but the Animal Isn't. Now What?

As previously stated, one of the hardest things for trainers to do is nothing. But there are times when nothing is precisely the thing to do! Nothing, that is, except take a deep breath and take note of what is going on around you. Here's what I mean.

When training goes well, we're ready to cheer, and that's great. Reinforce and move on to the next step in your behavior recipe. But when training goes poorly, we also want to take immediate action. We want to step in and fix it right away, often with the same zeal as when we reinforce. Right idea. Wrong time.

For the moment, let's assume we have preplanned our session. We've controlled the environment as much as possible to prevent accidental reinforcement in case things go astray, and we have a clear picture of what it is we want our animal to do at a given moment based on past training. That means we have a clear idea of the criteria we're looking for (i.e., duration, energy, frequency, and topography), we expect the animal to succeed, and we're planning to hold the animal accountable. Now, since we're clear on the criteria we're looking for, once the behavior occurs, we only have one decision to make—was the criteria met or not? The choice is black and white. Yes or no. Thumbs up or down. No maybes about it.

By now, it should be second nature to reinforce when the behavior criteria are met. But what if the behavior didn't meet the anticipated criteria? Traditional approaches tell the trainer to react, usually with punishment. So what options are available to reinforcement trainers? We certainly don't want to accidentally or deliberately reinforce any behavior that is below criteria.

This is where the skill of doing nothing comes into play. If the animal fails to meet your current criteria, you respond *by doing nothing* or as close to nothing as possible, for a few seconds immediately after its response. It doesn't need to be a long pause, just 3 to 5 seconds max. This is known as a Least Reinforcing Scenario or LRS.[5]

Notice the word reinforcing. You may be wondering why anyone would reinforce when the animal fails to meet the criteria or displays some unwanted behavior. The important word in LRS is *least*, which means we're doing the thing that offers the smallest amount of reinforcement possible when the animal fails to do what we ask. This is why it's important to make sure you completely control the animal's environment and her access to reinforcement. The goal is to communicate to the animal that, while you appreciate her coming back calmly to try again, the last response was not up to par and there will be a momentary pause in the delivery of reinforcement. However, the LRS does *not* mean to stand there with your arms folded, staring at your animal while you seethe with rage wanting to scream, "You got it wrong!" The LRS is a relaxed, non-reaction to your animal and a non-reinforcement of the behavior that wasn't quite up to the level you believe your pet is capable of at this moment.

The reason the Least Reinforcing Scenario is able to reduce, even eliminate, an unwanted response is due to a process called *extinction.* In behavioral terms, the extinction of a response occurs when a behavior that was previously reinforced stops being reinforced. When the animal recognizes that there is no benefit to the response—no more treats, toys, or praise—it will gradually stop offering the response. Eventually, the response may fade out all together. But deliberately extinguishing a well known, unwanted behavior takes patience. Any accidental reinforcement of the response can set the extinction process way back and even make the unwanted behavior stronger than when you started! In fact, one of the most common mistakes people make in training is to react prematurely to a behavior undergoing extinction. Getting into the habit of using the LRS can prevent us from making the mistake of reinforcing unwanted behaviors.

The LRS is a clever tool to help trainers respond to their animal's unwanted behavior in a way that doesn't make the problem worse. Once the animal understands that when you use the LRS punishment is not imminent, a set of really useful behaviors usually comes about. These include making good eye contact, returning to station, showing a relaxed posture, tail wagging, and paying attention to the trainer. Why does this happen? For one thing, the animal quickly learns that it does not need to fear punishment if it makes a mistake, which leaves it free to respond in a calm manner. Thus, each of these useful behaviors should be randomly reinforced after your 3 to 5 second pause. Doing so teaches an animal how to respond appropriately even after missing the mark. In other words, using an LRS helps shape an animal to be ready and willing to go again. It results in an animal that lacks fear and develops confidence in itself and the trainer, even as it makes a few mistakes along the way.

So does using the LRS mean the animal is reinforced for failure? Not at all! Following the LRS pause, the animal receives variable reinforcement for calmly accepting that pause. In practice, the specific behavior(s) that get reinforced at the end of the pause will depend on you. For instance, I prefer an animal to come back to station, give me eye contact, and show it's ready for the next request, without displaying avoidance, excessive frustration, or worse, aggression, towards me.

Don't be confused. Consistent application of the LRS following incorrect behaviors won't train that new behavior you're working on. But it will help teach the animal the difference between what are correct criteria and what are not, in a manner that avoids using any punishment. This is perhaps its best feature. It's an opportunity for you to cool off instead of unleashing your frustration on your student. It also buys you time in the heat of the moment to process what you should do next. For example, after witnessing a below criteria behavior (and reacting with an LRS), should you ask for the same behavior again, go on to something new, or end the session? If you elect to go on, the LRS gives you an instant to decide what the next behavior request should be.

The Difference Between "No!" and the LRS

You may be wondering how the LRS differs from using the word "No" or "Wrong." After all, doesn't "No" at some level convey that a behavior isn't meeting criteria? Why not just use "No"?

Using "No" (or some variation of it such as "Wrong," "Cht," "Ah, ah, ah" or "@#$%-it!") in the usual sense is a form of punishment. Actually, it's a sound with no meaning whatsoever until it's accompanied by some sort of unpleasant consequence like a stern voice, a penny can, a rolled newspaper swat on the hind end, a jerk of the leash, a choke or prong collar, an electric shock, etc. Punishment in all its forms does decrease the odds that the behavior it follows will occur again, which is why its use is popular, although misguided. The problem is "No" gets a little dull after a while and eventually that sound isn't as scary to the animal as it used to be. So "No" becomes, "No... I said no" and then, "No, No, NO!" All the while that little word becomes less effective at stopping the unwanted behavior. Then there's the question of the effectiveness or wisdom, not to mention the ethics, of using punishment on animals, especially large ones. A wise trainer I knew summed it up this way, "You can't spank a killer whale!"

At some point, traditional trainers have a choice: escalate the form of punishment to make "No" more effective again or live with the unwanted, problem behavior. Neither outcome is tolerable or necessary.

The Least Reinforcing Scenario alleviates the need to punish. Remember that as a trainer, you control most if not all the reinforcement available. If that's not currently the case for your situation, it's vital that you increase your control over your animal's environment so you can better guide its learning and its behavior. When you control the environment and use the LRS, the unwanted behavior will fade due to the minimal reinforcement coming from you or the surroundings. In contrast, if you react to your animal immediately as it displays an unwanted response instead of using the LRS, you risk inadvertently reinforcing the unwanted behavior just by paying attention to it!

Think about it from the animal's perspective. Suppose you respond to your pet at the instant it does something you don't want to see happen again, such as barking incessantly. Usually, since life with you is about reinforcement, a pet hearing its name may think it's about to receive more reinforcement. This is true even if the sight of you, the usual source of its reinforcement, is then followed by a punishment such as a stern yell, a pop of the leash, or worse. By reacting to your pet as it barks, the unwanted behavior was *first* met with something resembling reinforcement! We know that behaviors that are reinforced will happen again, and again, and again... Now, I'm betting that, "good job, do it again" is not the message you intended to convey at the moment your dog is singing at the top of his lungs. Just imagine the confusion you create when a pet must guess whether you're calling its name to praise it or to punish it. Even if the sight of you isn't all that reinforcing to your animal, chances are still high that you've changed its environment enough to accidentally reinforce the unwanted behavior anyway.

A barking dog is a classic problem and, out of frustration, most of us have probably resorted to yelling at a barking dog at one time or another. Like all punishments, yelling can stop the behavior momentarily, often until you close the door and get settled comfortably back in your chair. Then the barking resumes. So why does this annoying behavior persist, even after you frequently punish it? Two reasons. First, punishment is only effective at stopping behaviors when the punishment, or the threat of it, is actually present. Second, the animal has learned that sometimes barking his fool head off gains access to some kind of reinforcement, like a moment of attention from you. Unfortunately, just because you can momentarily stop a behavior with a punishment doesn't mean you've addressed the underlying cause for the behavior. Until you address the motivation behind the unwanted behavior, it will probably occur again.

If this is your situation, don't wait until your animal is so bored, hot, hungry, thirsty, or just in need of some attention that it's learned to howl the doggy blues. Get off your chair during the commercials while the animal is acting appropriately, such as being quiet, and reinforce that desirable behavior. The lasting difference that results when you're being proactive and randomly *reinforcing them before they fail*, compared to when you're being lazy and reacting with punishment after they fail, will amaze you and please your neighbors.

Teaching an animal what it shouldn't do is a lot harder than teaching it what it should do to gain reinforcement in the first place.

I recall the stunned looks by several participants at a training workshop years ago when I suggested a good way to ensure that your dog will sleep quietly through the night is to occasionally make the effort to reinforce it during the wee hours. I wouldn't take this so far as to suggest setting the alarm clock. But if you happened to be up anyway getting a glass of water or heading to the bathroom, why not reward your pets for doing just what you want—sleeping silently through the night—even if you first have to wake them up? It's much more effective than throwing an old shoe at them after they have begun howling in the moonlight.

An LRS Audit

Criticism of the Least Reinforcing Scenario often overlooks one of the most beneficial aspects of this training concept. Of course the 3 to 5 second LRS pause has a desirable effect on animal behavior over the long run by teaching animals to calmly accept minimal reinforcement following unwanted responses. But more importantly, the LRS helps prevent trainers from making things worse by stopping us from accidentally reinforcing or purposefully punishing a poor behavior. Furthermore, the advent of the LRS has the added benefit of forcing the trainer to make the tough decision: does the response meet the current criteria? Yes? Great! Reinforce it. Not quite? No problem. Use an LRS and move on. It's that simple. The alternative is an indecisive trainer who is unclear in his or her expectations and who will end up shaping an animal that displays mediocre behavior criteria. This happens because the animal is confused by the trainer's inability to consistently communicate standards without resorting to punishment.

During your first encounters using the LRS, you may struggle a bit over exactly how and when to use it. You aren't alone. To this day, there seems to be no end to the debate over how to carefully, consistently, and correctly offer an LRS in all situations.

Is there a fixed posture trainers should maintain to communicate the LRS? How long should I wait for the unwanted response to terminate or for the animal to return to me? Seconds, minutes, hours? When exactly does the LRS begin? At the point of failure, with the completion of the entire behavior, or when reinforcement is typically offered?

The truth is, much of this debate is just hairsplitting. So don't fret about it. We can probably never be absolutely neutral in response to our animal's missteps—after all, life offers continuous stimuli and experiences. *But for animals that have been taught to understand the concept that variety is itself reinforcing, we can do our best not to add to reinforcement that may already be present by striving to minimize any changes in those critical few seconds following an unwanted behavioral response.* It's during those few seconds immediately following any response, wanted or not, that the strongest associations are made and learning occurs. If we con-

Introduced nearly two decades ago, use of the LRS is widespread among trainers of more species than ever before.

sistently use the LRS, we'll avoid encouraging our animals to learn the things we don't want them to repeat.

Conversely, the ever-present use of "No" in behavior circles, with all the trappings of punishment we've discussed, encourages the trainer to respond to the failure immediately. The LRS demands the opposite by simply seeking to minimize reinforcement including our reactions. As a result, the LRS is often not specific about what part of the behavior was not up to criteria. It is a sort of behavioral "uncertainty principle"—it communicates that some aspect of the behavior wasn't met. But, trainers have no way of showing the animal exactly where the behavior broke down *at the moment it occurs*, without risking reinforcing it. For some of us, this aspect of the LRS can be extremely frustrating.

Here's an example. A wonderful trainer I know has a tough time accepting this limitation and it's no wonder. We'd all *like* to be able to "fix" behaviors the moment they stray off course. This trainer is on board with reinforcing desirable behavior, but she questions how the animal is supposed to understand when, where, and at what point in the behavior it failed. She wants to be able to pinpoint for the animal exactly when it strays off course, so to speak. In most cases, that's asking too much of the LRS. And for the trainer, it's looking backward at the mistake when the focus should be forward. Failure has already occurred; you can't undo it. However, you can prevent the unwanted approximation from getting stronger in the future by responding with an LRS right now. The LRS is simply a brief pause in the action designed to prevent inadvertent reinforcement of a sub par behavior. While it helps prevent behaviors from getting worse, it won't automatically fix one that has fallen apart. Repairing aspects of a long or complex behavior, whether the problem lies at the beginning, middle, or end, means going back to your behavior recipe at a later date and putting in some session time to help the animal recall what it is you expect. Break the deteriorating behavior down into smaller steps and spend future sessions reminding the animal how to be successful at each approximation—a "behavior tune up" so to speak. And above all, you must reinforce the approximation that needed improvement once you get it. Then you'll be able to put it all back together into the more complex behavior once the animal remembers all the small steps along the way. Remember: no single session conditions a behavior forever, and no one session can break it.

No Need for "No!"

Some trainers like to think they can speed the training process along by skipping the LRS. Rather than concentrating on success, they try to show the animal exactly what it's doing wrong by immediately punishing mistakes with a stern "No" or worse. This often requires a leash in order to perform the correction. Make no mistake; a correction like this is a form of punishment—it conveys, "Stop what you are doing." These trainers then offer a "good doggie" or some other feeble bridge immediately following the punishment. But how reinforcing do you suppose those words are after a while, particularly when repeated over again with no significant reinforcement such as a toy, food item, or scratch behind the ears? Think how confusing this rapid fire "she loves me, she loves me not, he loves me, he loves me not..." practice must appear from the animal's point of view.

Still others will go so far as to set their animal up for failure just so they can then apply a correction. It sounds unbelievable, but it's true. How much sense does it make to practice mistakes? Do star running backs practice fumbling the football? Does a gymnast rehearse a bad landing? Of course not! If you practice your mistakes, you are liable to become good at making them, and that's true for your animals as well. In contrast, champions always attempt to model the very behavior they aspire to achieve.

An all too common situation where a correction is typically used is while walking a dog that pulls on the leash. Before you fall into the trap of applying corrections, ask yourself what is causing this unwanted behavior? If a dog is tugging on the lead there are only two possible causes: it's running to something it wants (reinforcement) or from something or *someone* it doesn't want (punishment). If this is happening to you, how does it feel knowing you are either boring, scary, or both to your pet? It's not a solution to "pop" the dog with its leash (punishment) whenever it pulls. The answer is to give your animal a reason to voluntarily stay by your side as you both walk, run, or stop. The truth is if you're dull, your animal will want to wander in search of his own reinforcement. If you punish your pet when you call, correct, or jerk it back to your side, you're only adding to your own lack of appeal to your animal.

Finally, consider this: just because some training device or technique is marketed to cut corners and accommodate your busy schedule, as opposed to working with your animal's unique learning pace, doesn't mean it's appropriate to use. There's no doubt such punishments can be temporarily effective at forcibly changing an animal's path. But what is the cost to you, your pet, and your relationship based on trust? Furthermore, how would you jerk a five-ton elephant across the floor in order to correct it? You can't. So why should it be considered an acceptable practice when applied to a dog, cat, or any creature simply because you are physically stronger than it is? Using leash corrections can cause serious injury, even death. Furthermore, it is lazy training and not consistently reliable. It's also not acceptable, especially since there is a viable alternative. Reason, patience, a little planning, some positive reinforcement and if necessary, an LRS can accomplish the same goals in a healthier, more productive way.

How *not* to catch
a kangaroo

ZOOMILITY 501

I can't emphasize enough the importance of having a flexible plan in mind before you interact with any animal. It doesn't have to be complicated, but it should be able to answer a few simple questions like: what am I looking for from this animal today, what am I going to do to get it, and what am I going to do once I do get it? Here's an example of what can happen when you go in without a plan.

As a keeper I appreciate all species, even the creepy looking ones. But the truth is I have had some of the most fun with kangaroos and wallabies. Perhaps hand-raising several young joeys has had something to do with it. However, not all of my encounters have been suitable for public consumption. Shortly after opening a four acre Australian exhibit, one of our zoo's gray kangaroos proved all the experts wrong by demonstrating that 'roos really can swim. I suspect it was probably more of a "hop-on-water" behavior—either way, a radio call stated that "a large kangaroo had made it across the exhibit moat, that he was cruising around the children's zoo, and could someone please put the animal back home?" Not your everyday call, so I decided to drop what I was doing to lend a hand.

Catching a kangaroo is sort of like steering a boat. You treat the tail like a rudder and direct him back home as he hops along. This is simple in theory, provided you can get a hold of the tail. You really don't want anything to do with the rest of the kangaroo—their powerful legs and sharp nails are a formidable defense.

Plus, why is it animals always seem to be faster than we think they are? Thinking (I use the term loosely) I had plenty of time to meet up with our wandering 'roo as he hopped towards the opposite end of the penguin exhibit located adjacent to the children's zoo, I decided to "cut him off at the pass." Thus, my first mistake was leaving the group of keepers that was following after him.

My second mistake was not having a clear picture in mind of what I was going to do once I had caught up with our friend from Down Under.

Working under the erroneous assumption that he must surely be lounging at the other end of the exhibit, I was confronted by the universal truth that animals are indeed faster than we think they are. I arrived at the narrow opening behind the penguins, and was startled to see nothing but kangaroo chest hairs. To this day, images of this meeting still flash through my mind. The beast stood about as tall as I did, completely filling my field of vision like a wide screen TV. Realizing I had only a split second before he cleaned my clock, I dropped to the ground muttering something along the lines of "Oh shoot." I would have gotten away with my momentary lapse (remember, the other keepers were at the other end of the exhibit), had it not been for the 20 or so guests lined up to board the nearby train ride, witnessing this odd version of leapfrog.

Eventually, thanks to the other keepers, the young kangaroo was safely coaxed back to his new home without any further problems, and the train riders quit their snickering. Over the next few days, as the 'roo became more desensitized to his new surroundings, he gave up on swimming and I swore off leapfrog.

Putting It All Together

Now that you've patiently read through more training information than you probably wanted to, it's finally time to put our plan together to teach a behavior. Training efficiently with the 3R's is really a matter of making the following quick and deliberate decisions:

- Select a behavior request based on the animal's current experience, knowledge, desensitization, and skill level.
- Determine whether that request is likely to be successful in the current situation (i.e., topography).
- Know what response you're looking for measured in terms of duration, energy, frequency, and/or topography.
- Judge whether that response was above or below current criteria.
- Choose an appropriate reinforcer for the correct response or offer an LRS for any response that was below criteria.
- Decide what to do next.

Got all that? Remember, you have to be quick, clear, and confident with these decisions. If you're not, imagine how confused your student will be. Do the best you can, realizing that it gets easier with practice.

OK. We've got it down on paper, but how do we get started? The good news is many of the behaviors we want animals to display are ones they already know. Our goal is to condition the animals to perform these common responses when and where we request them. So, for example, if you see your puppy is about ready to lower itself into a sitting posture, reinforce it. There's a training session, albeit a short one. But, it's a session nonetheless, and one with one hundred percent success. Next time it looks ready to sit, you might also introduce the request for "Sit" and reinforce it again. Now for the training enthusiast, capturing a few behaviors this way might seem like cheating, compared to a more deliberate process of training by approximation. On the other hand, why not use every advantage to teach your animals to be successful for simple behaviors they are doing anyway?

For new or very young animals with short attention spans, it's far better to have many shorter sessions (even ones instigated by the animal), than to have one long and boring session filled with failure, just because it fits your schedule. To satisfy most pet owner's behavior expectations, training an animal for life doesn't have to be complicated or laborious. It often just means being ready at a moment's notice to reinforce the animal for responses already displayed throughout the day.

The same argument can be made for zookeepers. Unlike trainers of companion animals, zookeepers working with wild animals often have limited training relationships due to the species, exhibit design, or the lack of resources such as time. Still, even a short-handed keeper staff can usually make considerable progress shaping constructive behaviors, like shifting animals on or off exhibit reliably, just by using the limited interactions available to them each day. You can do the same thing at home. Just make sure you're always ready for whatever your animals do by having reinforcers handy around the house, in the car, in the yard, in your pockets, or anywhere else you may end up interacting with your animals.

In addition to reinforcing behaviors animals do on their own initiative, trainers will want to design sessions to speed things along. So before you start with your animal, be sure to preplan the session as much as possible. For example, does the animal appear ready for a training session? Based upon the animal's past success, what do you expect to accomplish today? What approximations will you request? Where, when, and with what will you reinforce? Will this goal match whatever the animal seems to be capable of doing or wanting at this moment? Or, after assessing the animal's recent behaviors, should you select a different set of goals, up to and including not training today? Remember, as reinforcement trainers, there's very little point in conducting a session that has a low probability of success before it even begins.

So how do you increase your odds of successfully designing and executing a session? How do you decide or estimate what the animal's current behavior criteria is and more importantly, whether you can anticipate more or less criteria the next time you request it? These questions are sometimes tough to answer for each animal in every situation. The answers are based on a variety of factors including trainer experience, knowledge of the individual animal and its reinforcement history, and sometimes just plain old luck! Nonetheless, there are some obvious situations when we should rethink our session plan and take greater precautions. For example, if an animal is injured or ill, if we're working with only one animal in a group of animals, if animals are engaged in sexual contact or demonstrating aggression, or if we're working with a female and/or her young, trainers should adjust their expectations and use greater caution.

> **When is it OK to remind them? Offering a second request at the instant just before the animal usually quits a response on its own can help to extend the behavior to greater levels. Be ready to reinforce even small gains in criteria!**

Regardless of the current situation, sooner or later, trainers are faced with the question of how and when to "raise the bar" to advance learning. Criteria measured in terms of duration, energy, frequency, or topography that was once acceptable (i.e., reinforced) may no longer be adequate to the trainer. We need a little bit more effort from the animal.

If we do our part by simplifying approximations, making incremental adjustments to our expectations, and using a variety of reinforcers, the animal should have little trouble sitting a few seconds longer, running a few seconds faster, jumping a fraction of an inch higher, etc. As a guide, pick a percentage of success the animal must reach

> **Reminder requests can be much softer or smaller than the origina request. Use only the signal necessary to encourage the animal to achieve a bit more than before. Second requests should be faded from use as soon as they are introduced.**

before you purposefully raise the criteria. For example, if your animal can sit at home alone with few distractions for exactly 1 minute before it gets bored and walks away at least 75 percent of the time, you could argue that the animal's duration criteria for a sit is just shy of 1 minute *in that topography*. However, if you ask for a sit in a crowded dog park, chances are it won't be able to sit for a whole minute—not even close. Since you've raised the criteria you expect by making the topography more complex, your best bet is to lower the duration of time you ask it to sit with all the distractions the park presents. Why? Your immediate goal is a quick respose to your request to sit despite the increase in temptations presented by the dog park. Thus, you are training an approximation designed to improve the animal's ability to respond quickly and correctly in new topographies. You are not working to extend the behavior's duration at the same time.

> **Use the four categories to measure behavior (duration, energy, frequency, and topography) to vary the type of approximations you request.**

Of course, in future sessions, you *will* be able to increase the duration they sit while at the dog park, because you are also going to teach them to extend the sit duration well past one minute back home, where things are familiar and less distracting.

Advancing behaviors quickly by knowing when to ask for more criteria and when to back off a bit takes practice. We've all felt like we're stuck in a training rut at one time or another. Often this occurs because trainers attempt approximations that are too complex for animals to understand. On top of that, animals sometimes forget behaviors! This is perfectly normal, but it also helps to explain why the training progress is sometimes slower than we'd like. So if your animal seems stuck or unable to grasp a certain step in a behavior, reinforce him for trying and take a break. Then go back to your list of approximations and simplify the ones he has trouble with before the next session.

> **Avoid using reminder requests *after* the animal has already begun to fail! Instead, only give quiet reminders while he is still succeeding.**

Also, when you begin a session, back up a few steps to an approximation the animal can easily complete—one that almost guarantees you will be able to reinforce. This will help remind him of what it is you're looking for and will start the session off with success. Then, based upon your pre-planning, you can ask for your next approximations that stretch the behavior a little bit more in one of the categories we've discussed: duration, energy, frequency, or topography. Again, in the beginning, avoid working two or more of these categories at the same time! Instead, reinforce progress in one area such as duration. Then switch to another aspect of the behavior that needs work in the next session.

Almost immediately as the animal begins to understand *how* to learn from you using the 3R's, you'll notice that training new behaviors is slightly different from maintaining old, familiar ones. For one thing, as a behavior becomes more reliable, the individual approximations don't need as much attention as they once did. Soon many steps can be combined into fewer ones until finally, only the completed behavior is reinforced—most of the time.

> **Training by approximations means assessing what the animal can do right now (not what it might have done yesterday) and building a little more from that point each day.**

Of course, to maintain the quality of the complete behavior forever, you'll still want to purposefully reinforce each step of that complex behavior from time to time. For instance, suppose your pet has learned to reliably stay in one location for several minutes. But lately, you've noticed that she's started to hesitate a second or two longer before responding to your request. What can you do to ensure the animal always responds quickly, without hesitation in the future? The simple answer is to be ready to immediately reinforce the animal for zero hesitation the very next time she doesn't hesitate! If you're looking to improve the start of a behavior (i.e., zero hesitation to a request), don't wait for or require her to complete the entire behavior (i.e., stay still for several minutes). Instead, seize the opportunity to instantly

> **Session Planning Tip: Are the new behaviors you plan to reinforce today compatible with each other or do they foster confusion? Avoid teaching new behaviors in the same session that oppose one another (e.g., "come here" vs. "go away").**

bridge and reinforce for an exceptionally quick response at the beginning of the behavior. You can always reward the full stay behavior at a later time.

Once a new behavior becomes a reliable one, trainers must still selectively reinforce not just the end, but also the beginning and middle, in order to maintain the quality of the entire response. (Think back to my story of the slow dolphin pick up on page 30.) Don't worry. Reinforcing them early once in a while just to maintain a known behavior's integrity won't break it!

Common Behavior Recipes

The training examples, or recipes, in the next section were selected for their usefulness, their similarity across different species, and their role in shaping more complex behaviors. Some may be more or less applicable to your situation, but all can be modified as needed. These recipes are based on a few assumptions. The first and most important is that you are only using positive reinforcement in your training. If you resort to punishment, even infrequently, you will have mixed results at best. In order for many of these common behaviors to become rock solid, your animal must completely trust you—and vice versa! As we've discussed, using punishment will only undermine that trust and result in failure for both of you.

The second assumption is that you're working with a relatively young or naïve animal. By naïve, I mean an animal that has a limited training history, such as a puppy or even a wild zoo animal. It presumes the animal has little or no past experience of punishment from you or anyone else. If your situation does not quite meet the second assumption, you'll probably need to do some extra work to overcome those previous learning experiences. You can do this through desensitization training using positive reinforcement. Yes, even if your animal has been previously punished, you can still turn things around. The second part of *Zoomility* addresses the specific case of animals with a history of punishment training, and the unique challenges trainers face to improve the quality of their relationship with their animals.

For now, take a look at the following behavior recipes designed to help you start training using only positive reinforcement. Use them as a starting point. Trainers should feel free to simplify or accelerate the steps as needed to meet their individual circumstances and training style as well as the experience level of the animal. Once the animal understands the behavior you're attempting to teach, you'll begin to shift from training a new behavior to maintaining an old one. Of course you'll still use the 3R's to maintain and strengthen known behaviors, but you'll also be able to combine many of the steps into larger, more complex ones.

To Help Organize Your Training Sessions, Each Behavior Recipe Follows This Format:

The behavior to be trained or problem to be solved.

Objective: The specific behavior we want to accomplish when the training is complete. If you don't know the objective, your animal won't understand what you want either.

Desensitization Required: The steps you need to take to get animals ready to start training. Assess your animals' current level of learning. Has their previous experience prepared them well enough to begin this new training? Many behaviors require animals to interact in some manner with people, places, and/or things. For example, an animal isn't likely to succeed at crate training if it is afraid of the crate. Thus, to achieve lasting success it is imperative that animals are taught to be at ease with these new objects, people, or places before they are expected to learn a new behavior.

Suggested Foundation Behaviors: These are basic skills the animal should have before beginning to learn a more complex behavior. Depending on the complexity of the behavior you plan to teach, it can be extremely helpful if the animal already understands the related foundation behaviors. They include simple behaviors such as sit, stay, down, and come. Teaching these behaviors first can result in a more efficient training session because there's less chance of confusing the animal with approximations that are too complex for you to easily communicate and for it to understand.

Request: The cue or cues that emit the behavior as it exists right now, and the cue you want to use in the future. When you select a cue or request to associate with the behavior you seek, be sure it's appropriate for the species you're training. Obviously, it doesn't make sense to choose a visual cue for an animal that's blind, or a spoken word cue for an animal that's deaf. Each behavior recipe offers suggestions to help you decide on your requests.

Response: The response section describes the four categories used to measure behaviors, as well as the relative importance of each to the behavior you're attempting to teach:

72

Duration measures the length of time of a response.

Energy measures whether the response should be vigorous or calm.

Frequency describes how often a response is to be repeated.

Topography describes the look of a response in relation to the physical environment in which it is performed.

Knowing exactly what you want the animals to do and how you will measure their progress each day is critical to training efficiently. Training often involves a little educated guesswork as you decide where to resume training from one session to the next. Be reasonable in your criteria expectations. If you happen to overestimate an animal's ability to complete an approximation one day, come back to that behavior component at a later time. Avoid chasing lower (and lower) criteria just to salvage a training session or to make a point. Zoomility is about knowing when to walk away and start fresh later—without holding a grudge.

Reinforce: Reinforcement is the reward we give to our animals. It's the key to teaching animals to be successful anywhere and everywhere, anytime and every time. This portion of the behavior recipe is by far the most important aspect for successful animal training. How we react to behavior determines whether that response is more or less likely to be repeated in the future. This fact should encourage us as trainers to pay attention to the details of reinforcement. Think about how, when, whether, and with what to reinforce in order to achieve crisp criteria and avoid spinning your wheels. Planning the timing and placement of reinforcement to match the concept you're trying to teach will help shape the response you want and get you there faster.

Concurrent Behaviors to Avoid: These are behaviors that should not be included in the same training session along with the objective behavior we're working toward. One reason? Animals cannot tell the difference between session time, playtime, and all other times of the day. To them, it's just time spent with you or without you. In the same way, animals can't tell when we've moved on from training a certain behavior one minute to training something else the next—particularly if those behaviors communicate very different objectives such as come here and go away. So where appropriate, each recipe has a section of behaviors to avoid training concurrently. This will help ensure that the objectives we've set and the placement of our reinforcements don't create confusion or delay achieving our goals.

Finally, for those of you who are new to training,

don't worry about making mistakes—you're going to make them all the time! My philosophy is that if I get through a training day without making more than a few mistakes, it's been a great day. The key is to stick to the plan: relax, have some fun, control the animal's environment as much as possible, reinforce only the criteria you want repeated, avoid resorting to punishment, and when needed, use an LRS (Least Reinforcing Scenario) to prevent accidental reinforcement of *your mistakes*. Remember, if an animal fails at an approximation, it's not the animal's fault. It's our responsibility because we put them in a learning situation for which they were not prepared to succeed. Good training isn't about shaping perfect animal behavior; it's about creating reliability, confidence, and trust when life doesn't go quite as planned.

Most of all, if you take nothing else from *Zoomility*, remember this: reinforce more, request less, and punish not at all. You'll be amazed at the results.

Desensitization
My animal is afraid of everything!

Objective: To teach an animal to completely and confidently ignore new or frightening objects, events, people, animals, activities, locations, sounds, smells, tastes, and tactile sensations. This is known as desensitization training and it includes anything that may cause the animal mental or physical discomfort, such as a trip to the veterinarian's office, loud noises, car rides, strangers, children, other animals, and so on. This non-fearful response will be the foundation for all successful future behavior training.

Desensitization Required: Desensitization is the point of this training recipe. This kind of training can and should continue throughout an animal's lifetime no matter what species or breed you have. Every new situation the animal encounters is a potential desensitization opportunity for trainers to use—don't take these experiences for granted or assume the animal will learn to cope on its own.

Suggested Foundation Behaviors: Start by building trust between yourself and the animal. Trainers of newly acquired, young, fearful, or inexperienced animals often have to work with a limited selection of reinforcements. So give first priority to finding new, effective reinforcers such as favorite food items, toys, and activities in order to build trust between the animal and yourself. *At this early stage of training, when your relationship is just beginning to form, try to reinforce more and request less.*

Request: You can't request an animal to be afraid or not be afraid. Instead, remember that everyday objects and events can and do have a profound effect on behaviors. Thus, every new experience is an opportunity for trainers to shape calm, confident animals under all conditions.

Response: In this case, you're really looking for a non-response. Animals that are desensitized show no physical reaction to changing conditions. For example, breathing rates don't increase, muscles remained relaxed, and animals don't back away from approaching objects, sounds, and other sensations (i.e., showing avoidance). In addition, behaviors aren't terminated early, requests are not refused, criteria don't decrease, and animals don't become fearful or aggressive.

Duration: A completely desensitized animal can remain calm for an extended amount of time no matter what new potentially aversive stimuli are present. Remember that it's not enough to help your animal get used to something at a distance. There's a huge difference between a big scary dog living a few houses away separated by fences, and one straying into your pet's backyard.

Energy: Generally, trainers should look for and reinforce calm, low intensity responses to new situations. Good indicators of relaxation are regular breathing, relaxed muscles, and normal eye contact. Wide-open eyes, excessive panting, or trembling bodies suggest anything but a calm animal.

Frequency: Since desensitization is about reinforcing the absence of a reaction from the animal, frequency is not as important an element of desensitization training.

Topography: The topography is the physical environment around the animal. If your animal is nervous about being in a new location or about changes to its usual surroundings, you may need to desensitize the animal to the topography. Animals often discriminate between familiar environments such as the home, and unfamiliar places and situations like a park, a new exhibit, being placed in a strange social group, or a trip to the veterinarian's office. As a result, trained behaviors that can easily be performed "at home" may seem to be impossible to perform in new situations. If animals do manage to respond, the behavior's criteria are often much lower than normal. To reduce these phenomena, trainers should actively approximate increasingly complex situations by introducing the animal to many new locations and experiences. Be sure only to apply reinforcement to the animal for *not* reacting to these changing events.

Reinforce: Take advantage of any and all changing conditions by *immediately* reinforcing animals for their *calm responses* to new situations. However, be very careful not to immediately react to stressful responses. Be selective. If the animal's initial reaction is startled, vocal, or one of fear and avoidance, wait a few seconds or more. Offer a Least Reinforcing Scenario (LRS) until the unwanted responses decrease and a more calm response such as regular breathing or relaxed muscles begins. Then reinforce increasing amounts of calm, desirable responses.

Whenever possible, trainers should also be prepared to reinforce the animal's calm responses to changes that naturally occur in the real world, such as an advancing thunderstorm, the approach of a mail-carrier, or the increasing volume of a distant siren. In these circumstances, it is often helpful to provide animals extra instructions prior to the expected change in the environment. Remember, the topography is about to radically change (e.g., loud thunder clap), so you may need to lower your criteria just a bit in other ways in order to ensure your animal's success. For example, you can request that the animal continues to "stay" or "sit" before an approaching guest presses the doorbell or at the flash of lightning before a thunder clap. Giving them a reminder request can help animals ignore the impending distraction a little longer because they know the request will be followed by reinforcement. The point is to not get greedy and expect the animal to perform as well as it would if the distraction wasn't present. Try to approximate just a little bit more success in the face of these environmental changes and then reinforce it.

Concurrent Behaviors to Avoid: None

New Reinforcers
How do I teach my animal to
prefer things other than just food?

Objective: To teach an animal to find objects like new toys, as well as events, people, animals, activities, behaviors, locations, sounds, smells, tastes, and tactile sensations to be reinforcing. Something is deemed reinforcing if it increases the probability of the preceding behavior occurring again. Reinforcements that are learned are called conditioned reinforcers.

Desensitization Required: Before something can be taught to be reinforcing, trainers should be certain animals are not afraid of the item intended to become a reward. Introduce new items slowly to see if the animals display interest or avoidance. If animals seem fearful, go back to the previous behavior recipe.

Suggested Foundation Behaviors: None

Request: Start by requesting or encouraging the animal to interact with the new reinforcer such as a toy. Typically, just giving the item to the animal will act as this request.

Response: Initially, you should look for animals to approach the new reinforcer, especially if that reinforcer is radically different from anything it has previously encountered. Avoid applying any other form of reinforcement if the animal backs away or ignores the new reinforcer.

Duration: Initially, trainers may simply need to reinforce timid animals for making eye contact with or briefly touching the new object. Plus, a good rule to follow to keep any reinforcer from losing its value is to remove it from the animal's environment *before* the animal becomes bored and leaves it. Think of the impact that reinforcer will have *the next time you offer it* if it's removed while the animal still shows some interest now, compared to if it's put away after the animal gets tired of it.

Energy: Animals should be reinforced for appropriate responses depending on the nature of the reinforcer used. Disposable conditioned reinforcers are often designed for clawing, chewing, swatting, or throwing. Others, such as petting or social companions require the animal to respond gently or with their mouths closed.

Frequency: Avoid using the same reinforcer repeatedly or predictably in training scenarios. Variety rules!

Topography: Without becoming predictable, try to match the reinforcer to the behavior and the environment. For example, some trainers use a gentle tap on the animal's body as a bridge. A firm pat on its side may be reinforcing and appropriate for some animals during an energetic exercise when the animal can tense its muscles in anticipation, but that same reinforcer may be counterproductive during a voluntary blood draw or nail clipping when the animal needs to be calm, stationary, and relaxed. In this case, a calm massage or soothing voice might be more appropriate.

Reinforce: Most conditioned reinforcers could stand to be "recharged" once in a while. The most effective way to keep something reinforcing is to follow it up with something else that is also reinforcing. Thus, new reinforcers are taught by following them with familiar reinforcement such as food, toys, or praise. The order of presentation is important! New reinforcement is always followed by known. As we'll explore with the retrieval behavior that follows on page 106, it's helpful to frequently reinforce animals for returning with and releasing toys back to the trainer with primary reinforcement.

Concurrent Behaviors to Avoid: None

Bridge

How do I tell my animal the instant
it's doing exactly what I want?

Objective: To teach an animal to recognize a special conditioned reinforcer called a bridge. A bridge can be a visual or audible cue or a touch that lets the animal know it has completed a desirable behavior and that more reinforcement will be coming when the animal returns to the trainer. The bridge teaches the animal to accept a brief delay between the completion of the response and the delivery of more meaningful reinforcement.

Desensitization Required: Trainers must be certain animals are not afraid of items or actions intended to become conditioned reinforcements.

Suggested Foundation Behaviors: None

Request: The bridge can be a consistent sound such as a whistle, clicker, or spoken word. It may also take other forms, such as a tap on the body or a point of the finger. Avoid overuse of the bridge or it will lose its value over time!

Response: The bridge signals the completion of the behavior and tells the animal that reinforcement is available, typically once the animal returns to the trainer.

> *Duration:* Trainers should have reasonable expectations for the time it takes the animal to return from a completed behavior. Animals will eventually learn to return quickly to the trainer to receive the actual reinforcement. However, on occasion, animals may become distracted or return slowly, especially if your bridge is weak due to overuse or lack of reinforcement. They may also respond slowly if the environment around them is more fun than your predictable reinforcements! If this happens, respond with the LRS (Least Reinforcing Scenario) and think about ways to make the bridge more motivating in the future.

> *Energy:* Since other reinforcers usually follow the bridge, animals will learn to hurry back to the trainer once it is conditioned. At the same time, you may wish to shape appropriate behaviors for the actual delivery of reinforcement following a bridge. For example, shaping them to calmly take a food item or ball from your hand is better than energetically munching your fingers along with that tasty treat.

> *Frequency:* The bridge is only as effective as the last time it was backed up with significant reinforcement. Remember the savings

80

account concept? You have to put in reinforcement in order for the bridge to have value later.

Topography: As with other conditioned reinforcers, it's good practice to match the reinforcer to the desired behavior. For instance, asking an animal to remain calm and motionless while you draw a voluntary blood sample is probably not the time to whistle loudly in its ear for a job well done.

Reinforce: To teach a bridge, simply present the bridge (e.g., "toot," "click," "Good," or tap on the body) and then follow it *immediately* with a known reinforcer. In the beginning, it may be helpful to use a favorite food item to cement the connection, but other reinforcers can and should be used to maintain the bridge after it's learned. Remember, the bridge is not a substitute for more meaningful reinforcement—it is only as strong as the last time it was reinforced.

Concurrent Behaviors to Avoid: None

Using a Target
How can I shape the behavior
responses I want using targets?

Objective: To teach an animal to gently touch its nose, forehead, or chin (depending on the species) to a physical target such as an open hand, object, or ball on the end of a stick, and to maintain that contact until instructed otherwise. Experienced animals can also be taught to touch other body parts such as hindquarters or feet to a target. Trainers can then move the target to guide the animal into various behaviors like sit, down, stay, and so on.

Desensitization Required: Animals must be familiar with *and unafraid* of the target object to be used. Additional desensitization training is necessary prior to target training if the animal shows avoidance of the proposed target. Such avoidance is indicated by behaviors including, but not limited to: the animal tenses its muscles or leans away from the object as it approaches its body, the animal purposefully walks around or runs from the object, or the animal vocalizes or widens its eyes as the object approaches.

Suggested Foundation Behaviors: Since targeting to the trainer's hand is often one of the first behaviors trainers teach their animals, few other conditioned behaviors are required. However, it's helpful if the animal is comfortably desensitized to the presence of the trainer, and will accept simple primary reinforcement (i.e., food) from him or her. A well-conditioned bridge can also be helpful, but it isn't absolutely necessary since reinforcement can be delivered quickly as the animal approaches/touches the target.

Request: The typical cue for targeting is the presentation of the actual target, whether it is the trainer's hand, a ball on the end of a pole, or a spot on the floor. As with all behavior requests, the target should be offered for a limited time only. Early on, if the animal accepts the request by physically moving closer to the target, then reinforce. If the request is completely ignored or the animal's response is too slow to meet your predetermined current criteria, temporarily remove the target and offer an LRS.

Response: Initially, trainers should look for and reinforce behaviors that suggest the animal is paying attention to the target, even if they don't quite understand what to do with it. For example, young or completely naïve animals may need to be reinforced for simply looking at the target. Other animals may quickly advance towards the target simply because it is something new to explore. It's not uncommon for animals to explore new objects with their mouths. Trainers should avoid accidental reinforcement of any mouthing of the target—while it is likely that the target itself will eventually gain reinforcing qualities of its own, it is not a chew toy!

Duration: For the finished behavior, animals should be able to gently touch and maintain contact with the target for a variable length of time until reinforced.

Energy: The final behavior should reflect an animal that is visibly calm, relaxed, and controlled in its movements. Avoid reinforcement of frustration behaviors like head bobbing, pushing on the target, mouthing, vocals, etc. The trainer, not the animal, determines where the target is placed, as well as when or if it is to be repositioned.

Frequency: Remember—the target is not a button on a vending machine the animal should push and release multiple times! If the animal jabs at the target rather than maintaining constant contact with it, wait for the animal to touch the target again and then reinforce. Eventually, the animal will understand that it's easier to remain in contact with the target than to repeatedly jab at it. Criteria for the finished behavior include making gentle contact with the target and maintaining that contact even as the target moves. As a result, frequency should not be a major component of targeting.

Topography: Animals are truly target trained when they are able to maintain contact with the target despite dramatic changes to their immediate environment, such as loud noises, arrival of new animals/people, and so on. Depending on the complexity of the session, remember to reduce your duration expectations as you increase the level of environmental distractions. As the animal learns to maintain contact under increasingly complex situations, trainers will be able to raise criteria on the duration of the target during these tougher conditions. Be reasonable. Add one distraction at a time and don't get greedy.

Reinforce: It's easy to teach the concept of "maintain contact with the target" no matter how the target moves by applying reinforcement only when the animal approaches and physically touches the target for increasing amounts of time in increasingly difficult situations. In other words, avoid reinforcing animals for jabbing and then backing away from the target. This can be accomplished by initially providing the reinforcement such as a food item, as if it comes from or immediately behind the target. If you're trying to manage both a target pole and reinforcement delivery with just two hands, you'll have an easier time if the animal first recognizes and responds to a bridge.

Concurrent Behaviors to Avoid: None

Elimination
How do I teach it when
and where to go potty?

Objective: To teach an animal the appropriate locations to eliminate.

Desensitization Required: Trainers should be aware of any avoidance response to unusual or unfamiliar surfaces such as concrete floors, newspapers, rubber mats, shavings, or grass. Desensitize as needed.

Suggested Foundation Behaviors: None. However, it is helpful to keep animals, especially young ones, on a feeding schedule. Plus, from a training perspective, I've never been a fan of feeding animals *ad lib* from an automated feeder or a giant bowl of food. You never know what sort of unwanted behaviors get randomly reinforced when animals have uncontrolled access to a bowl of food all day and night. Be consistent in the number of times you feed each day. Avoid switching from several feedings one day to just a few the next or quickly switching from predominantly A.M. feedings to P.M. ones. Also, feeding and drinking times should match your availability to observe puppies for signs they need to go, to take animals for a walk, or simply to let them outside. If your puppy's bowel or bladder is too small to enable it to sleep through the night, try limiting its access to food and water a few hours before bedtime. Otherwise, set your alarm clock for a midnight potty break until he gets a bit older and more successful making it through the night.

Request: Healthy animals are often very predictable with their potty habits. In fact, young animals such as puppies will often begin eliminating as soon as they finish eating or drinking. The reason is their maturing bodies automatically respond to eating/drinking by sending a signal to the other end that it is time to go—NOW. Therefore, *it makes absolutely no sense to punish a young animal for potty mistakes.* Their bodies simply have not matured to a level where they have voluntary control over their own bowel movements. The good news is trainers have an obvious opportunity to teach successful potty training every time the animal consumes water or food.

Response: As young animals finish eating or drinking, trainers should place the animal immediately wherever it is they wish the animal to learn to eliminate. For most of us, this will be outside the home on grass or dirt, but the same logic applies to animals expected to eliminate indoors on newspaper, for example. The key is to guarantee early success by being proactive. Sure, mistakes will still happen from time to time. But potty training does not need to take a long time to learn. If apartment animals must be kept inside to eliminate, try as much as possible to separate where they are expected to eat, sleep, and play from where they should "go." Animals will quickly understand the difference between "this is where I eat and sleep" versus "this is where I eliminate" as long as you give them plenty of opportunities to go.

When a mistake occurs because you waited too long to take them outside, clean up the mess without drawing any attention to it (i.e., LRS). Remember, the young animal is only responding to its body's autonomic response; it isn't trying to defy you! If circumstances prevent you from getting that new puppy outside or on paper frequently (e.g., once per hour during the day), limit his access to areas of the home such as carpeted rooms or near furniture where a mess will cause you to flip out. Instead, restrict him to areas of the home where, if he cannot hold it, a mess won't cause permanent stains or odors. A tile floor or exercise pen is a good choice.

Duration: There are two aspects of duration to consider here. The first and most important is learning to successfully extend the length of time between potty breaks. This aspect of the final behavior will easily and incrementally improve as their bodies develop, provided we show them where to succeed and give them every opportunity necessary.

The other duration aspect may surface as the animal matures and we have fallen into a daily routine. This duration is the length of time between when the potty break is offered and when the animal actually eliminates. Young animals may occasionally take a while longer to eliminate than adults and vice versa. In any case, think about reinforcing the animal for quickly eliminating as it matures and avoid predictably rushing them back inside once they do go. In other words, once they've finished going, spend some extra time reinforcing them before you rush off to start your day. This will help prevent you from inadvertently teaching an "end of session" signal that communicates to your animal that once they eliminate, fun time outside is over. Otherwise, some animals may learn to avoid eliminating right away (causing their owners to be late for work!), because eliminating quickly signals the end of reinforcement and the start of a long, boring, predictable day alone.

Energy: For young animals that are learning the concept of where and when to go, avoid excessive playtimes until after they make an effort to eliminate. Keep in mind that reinforcement such as playtime should always *follow* a desired behavior response; it doesn't come first.

Frequency: When it comes to potty training, it takes as long as it takes and as often as it takes. That said, prevention of mistakes in areas you don't want animals to go is entirely up to you, not your pet. As the animal matures and becomes reliable, you can slowly decrease the number of times you offer it a potty break by increasing the time between breaks.

Topography: It's not uncommon for animals to have difficulty going anywhere else if they've learned only to go in one location such as a concrete slab, inside the home, in a crate, on paper, or on grass. The more trainers can encourage animals to learn to eliminate in (or on) a variety of places, the easier time adult animals will have when they're held overnight in an unfamiliar clinic, kennel, or hotel. In our family's case, when we initially moved to a desert climate, my adult dogs had difficulty understanding where they should go since there was no longer any grass in their backyard!

Reinforce: Elimination is a type of behavior whose completion has an intrinsic reinforcement value of its own, regardless of anything the trainer does or does not do. If your circumstances often cause the animal to have accidents, confusion may soon develop. By eliminating in the "wrong place," the animal's bladder feels better, but it also knows you don't approve. So both successes and failures are reinforced, just from different sources. In this case, even previously reliable adult animals may develop a problem. Prevent mistakes by giving animals of all ages plenty of opportunities to go and be sure to provide praise and fun for a job well done.

Concurrent Behaviors to Avoid: None

Name Recall

How do I get my animal to come
to me when and where I ask?

Objective: To teach an animal to return to its trainer when its "name" is called.

Desensitization Required: Animals must be desensitized to people, or at least to the trainer teaching the recall.

Suggested Foundation Behaviors: It's helpful if the trainer has identified reinforcers a newly acquired animal prefers. Targeting can be helpful but isn't required to teach the recall behavior.

Request: Typically, an animal's spoken name (or some other sound) is the signal to return to the trainer. However, for species better suited to visual or tactile sensations, the learning process is the same—only the form of the request changes. For example, trainers of free flight birds often use visual signals, like an outstretched arm, instead of auditory cues while the animal is far away in flight.

Response: Upon hearing its name, the animal should immediately stop what it is doing and return to the trainer.

Duration: As with the bridge, the criterion for the time it takes to return is determined by the trainer. If you want your animal to return quickly and reliably every time, reinforce it every time. If the return was too slow, use an LRS and move on to the next behavior. You can always come back to this approximation later. Under no circumstance should you ever punish it for coming back, no matter what it may have just done. Otherwise, the return will likely be even slower next time.

Energy: A fast response is desirable but be certain to shape a little control, too, such as "sit in front of the trainer" after the animal makes its speedy approach back to you. Nobody likes to be knocked around unless you asked to be bowled over.

Frequency: Animals will learn to return as often as needed provided trainers make it fun and interesting for them.

Topography: Trainers working with an animal at a distance, especially if it's off lead, free swimming, free ranging, or free flying, will feel more at ease with a well-conditioned recall behavior. However, the greater the complexity you intend to expose the animal to, the less control you will have over reinforcements (and punishments) lurking in the environment. Thus, it is critical that trainers approximate increasingly complex scenarios and reward success with variable, frequent, and unpredictable reinforcements. Don't let the environment be more interesting than you are!

Reinforce: New, wild, or fearful animals may initially be unable or unwilling to approach a trainer close enough to accept primary reinforcement by hand. In that case, trainers may have to provide reinforcement when animals simply advance a little closer to them. For more experienced animals, providing variable reinforcement by hand is a natural progression of the recall behavior assuming trainers don't ever confuse the situation by also using punishment. Animals that have to guess whether the trainer is about to respond with reinforcement or punishment will either hesitate, return slowly, or refuse altogether. Look at it from their point of view; return quickly to station and possibly receive a punishment, or wander in search of reinforcement while attempting to avoid punishment at its source (i.e., you). *Prevent confusion: never punish.*

That said, even the most well-trained and reinforced animal may occasionally be motivated to explore what the environment has to offer, especially if we humans have been a bit boring lately. In those instances, trainers should quietly move in a direction slightly away from the animal. Here's why: let's assume you've preplanned the location of the session so that you're able to completely and safely ignore the animal if it doesn't meet criteria. In other words, its wandering won't get the animal into trouble, such as crossing a busy street. If the animal refuses to be recalled or heads off on its own, trainers should respond with the LRS and then move *away* from the animal. It's true that the animal may, momentarily, get reinforced by an unknown goodie such as an unfamiliar scent in the environment, but that's all it will get. The real source of reinforcement (you) isn't sticking around to further reinforce the animal for refusing to come when it is called. If the animal wants the trainer's attention, the animal needs to be attentive to what the trainer is doing and requesting. *As with all behavior requests, responding to a recall is a limited time offer!* If the animal isn't interested at that moment, fine. But don't reinforce them for ignoring you by chasing after them, or by repeating the request a dozen times. On the flip side, never punish them for poor return criteria when they finally do return. Instead, make it appear that you are ignoring them (all the while making certain they aren't headed for trouble or injury) by slowly walking away from them. When they do return, don't pay immediate attention to them. This will prevent you from accidentally reinforcing a slow, wandering return. Instead, offer an LRS. Then reinforce them for accepting the LRS and paying attention, and move on to the next behavior.

Of course, you should only do this if the risk to the animal or others is minimal. If it wanders in a crowded park or city street, calmly retrieve your animal without punishing it, reinforce it as little as possible, and think about simplifying future sessions. If the wandering persists, odds are you are boring or the situation you've placed them in is just too complex for them to handle without becoming distracted at this stage of their training. Make things easier by simplifying the topography in which you ask for the recall. Go back to a level that almost guarantees future success by reducing the number of distractions, using shorter session times, getting some new reinforcers, and most importantly, using them!

Concurrent Behaviors to Avoid: None

Crate Training
How do I get my animal to go into
an enclosure and remain calm?

Objective: To teach an animal to patiently and consistently enter and exit a pen, crate, horse trailer, yard, or other enclosure and to remain calmly inside for extended periods of time.

Desensitization Required: It might be helpful to introduce the enclosure with the door off or securely held open. Begin reinforcing the animal for approaching the exterior of the enclosure.

Suggested Foundation Behaviors: Sit or stay and a variety of known reinforcers, including a bridge, are helpful.

Request: This request can be an audible sound or a visual signal such as saying the word "Inside" or pointing a finger in the direction of the enclosure. However, unless you enjoy being knocked over, the act of opening the door to the enclosure should *not* be the cue. Often, we inadvertently teach animals that an open door (or the act of opening a door) is an invitation to do something like knock the trainer over as they run in or out. So unless you aren't too particular about your criteria, an opening or closing door, whether it is located on a kennel, car, crate, monkey exhibit, or house, should be the signal to do nothing!

Response: Consistent use of an enclosure such as a crate actually depends on several simple behaviors including stay, wait for the door to open or close, enter or exit as requested, and remain calm inside. Each component or foundation behavior needs to be taught, reinforced, and maintained. Failure to reinforce each step of the process may result in animals that either refuse to enter or race to exit enclosures of any kind.

Duration: Animals can learn to remain inside a pen for amazing lengths of time provided we reinforce them. The secret is to avoid predictability. In other words, don't just crate them when you will be gone for hours, and they have no access to new and variable reinforcers. Try crating them not just when you plan to leave, but also when you are home, at unpredictable times of the day, and for a few minutes rather than a few hours at a time. Be different. If you are playing, include the pen as one of the places animals can expect to have a lot of fun, receive reinforcement, and get attention from you. I've even known trainers that crawl inside travel crates with their animals.

Energy: Life inside any sized enclosure need not be dull. However, most of the time trainers should look for calm, quiet, low energy behaviors while animals are inside one. This is particularly true just prior to releasing them from a crate. Since even the most well-conditioned animals will eventually desire a change of scenery, it is important for the trainer to avoid accidentally reinforcing (negatively or positively) animals for excited, agitated, or escape-like behaviors just prior to the door opening.

Frequency: Trainers who reinforce well will have animals that eagerly enter and re-enter a pen even after spending a long duration inside.

Topography: The more interesting the world (or living room) outside the crate seems to your animal, the more challenging it will be to make being inside fun. Keep this in mind whenever you crate your animal during road trips to new, exciting, or possibly frightening locations. The new sites and sounds outside any enclosure may make time inside it even less appealing. You can help your animal succeed by reducing your duration expectations and/or increasing the frequency of your reinforcement while they are kenneled someplace new.

Reinforce: In order to maintain strong gating criteria, try placing reinforcement through one of the small openings along the backside to get it as far back in the crate (or horse trailer) as possible. This will give reinforcement to the animal while its head and body are facing the back, rather than when it's facing the door poised for escape. Animals that eagerly bolt from a pen should rarely, if ever, be positively reinforced upon exiting it. Remember, being inside a crate for hours can get boring, even aversive if they have to eliminate. So it's possible for animals to be negatively reinforced for "escaping" the kennel every time they exit one! To prevent escape-like behaviors, positively reinforce them before you let them exit, especially after a long duration inside the enclosure. It may help to ask (and reinforce) them to sit (or stay) before you approach them, reach for the door, turn the handle, or actually open the door. This will help you to avoid pairing "door is open" with their exit response. A moving or open door is not a signal to enter or exit.

Again, be certain to minimize any negative or positive reinforcement of avoidance behaviors. Unless you have that one unique animal that refuses your request to exit a kennel after being inside it all day, don't reinforce the animal for leaving the enclosure. While training animals to enter any enclosure, use small, frequent reinforcers. For example, use many quickly consumed treats rather than giving one large piece of hot dog that can be slowly enjoyed as the animal reverses course and reinforces itself for running *away* from the crate!

Finally, make sure you don't train the animal to

believe that when the door is shut, reinforcement is over. Unfortunately, this is often precisely what trainers inadvertently teach the animal as they head out the door to go to work all day or when zookeepers go home for the night. Instead, vary the duration of time the animal spends inside a crate, pen, trailer, or night house. Then, reinforce it in a manner that may appear random to the animal, but at a rate that systematically increases desirable behaviors while inside the enclosure. Another secret is to limit access to the enclosure when you don't want or need them to be inside. For example, as you prepare to release them, reinforce them for stationing quietly inside and for patiently waiting for you to open the door. Then ask them to exit, close the door, and end your interaction for a few minutes or more. In other words, don't positively reinforce them for escaping! This will help convey the concept that being inside is more fun than being outside. In essence, think of an enclosure as any other conditioned reinforcer; the less animals are satiated with it, the more reinforcing it will become. Treat any enclosure as "the fun place to be" by reinforcing animals often while they're inside one and by controlling access to it, when they are not. As a result of this approach, at the end of the day, my dog stands by the closed kennel door looking at me as if asking permission to go to bed.

Concurrent Behaviors to Avoid: None

Sit

How do I get my animal to sit when and where I want?

Objective: To teach an animal to keep all four paws on the ground with hindquarters lowered.

Desensitization Required: Animals should be desensitized to any surface where they will be asked to sit.

Suggested Foundation Behaviors: Targeting, a bridge, and a supply of conditioned reinforcers.

Request: Animals physically capable of sitting often do. Thus, it is never necessary to force an animal into a sit posture by pushing on its hind end. Simple targeting will suffice. If the animal has learned to follow a target with its nose or chin, simply raise the target up and back slightly towards the tail end of the animal. This should lift the animal's head and begin to lower the hind end—the beginnings of a sit. At some point, gravity will take over and the animal will likely finish the sit on its own without further need to target the head back further. It may be helpful to position the animal in front of a wall or on carpet to help it avoid moving backwards or slipping.

Response: Sitting is such a commonly displayed behavior for some species that trainers can make progress teaching animals to respond on request simply by reinforcing animals whenever they observe the animal sitting. This is reinforcement well spent, since learning to sit on cue is an important foundation behavior necessary for teaching many more complex behaviors.

Duration: Since many species rest by sitting, the length of time an animal can be conditioned to sit is almost limitless.

Energy: While sitting may be a low energy response, it is not a low criteria behavior. Animals should still exhibit attention to the trainer in anticipation of the next request.

Frequency: This is probably not as important as the other components. However, the sit usually has such a strong reinforcement history that frequent requests shouldn't be too difficult for the animal.

Topography: As you might expect, it is easier for animals to hold a sit position in comfortable, familiar, less distracting places. Trainers should anticipate that new, scary, or fascinating locations might affect an animal's ability to hold the duration of a sit for the same length of time as when there are no unusual distractions.

Reinforce: It's easy for trainers to take this ordinary behavior (and others like it) for granted by forgetting to reinforce it. In addition, over time, animals anticipating a trainer's predictable or careless reinforcement delivery often learn to break from the sit position and move forward to help the trainer get the reinforcement to them sooner! As with all behaviors, reinforcement placement can either strengthen or weaken the final product. For example, in order to maintain the integrity of the sit behavior, trainers should reinforce animals only when all four legs are making contact with the ground. Sometimes animals, especially young and tired puppies, may tend to slouch to one side if trainers aren't too mindful of their reinforcement habits. If that's all the criteria you need, fine. But for those of you who want a little more crispness to the sit, be aware of any slouching as you reinforce. One way you can reduce this is by delivering a reinforcer (food treats lend themselves well here) from the opposite direction of the slouch. For example, if the animal is resting on its back right hip and leg, offer reinforcement from its front left side just slightly out of normal reach. This will require the animal to reposition forward and to its left to reach slightly for the reinforcement. Thus, the animal will actually receive reinforcement for a proper sit with its weight equally distributed on its hind feet.

After you reinforce a sit, (or stay, heel, down) remember to reward yourself with a pat on the back. We rely on these everyday behaviors all the time, often without thinking much about their importance. So it's imperative to make the effort to reinforce your animal frequently for these transitional behaviors and to note for yourself when you remember to do it. There's also a common trainer error to avoid here. Don't assume your animals know what you expect them to do after you reinforce a sit. Remind them what it is you want them to do next! Why? Recall the 3R's. The act of reinforcing them communicates, "Good job, mission accomplished, my request has been satisfied." If you sometimes want them to continue the same behavior and other times you want to move on to something else, how are they supposed to know the difference? Should they keep sitting or follow after you? Whatever response you desire next, after reinforcement is delivered, make certain you request it. Animals are clever, but it's unfair to expect them to read your mind. Be clear, and together you will both succeed.

Concurrent Behaviors to Avoid: None

Stay

How do I teach my animal to stay put even if I leave the area?

Objective: To teach an animal to remain completely still whether standing, sitting, or lying down until instructed otherwise.

Desensitization Required: Animals may need to be desensitized to unfamiliar objects, sounds, etc. as more complex topographies are approximated.

Suggested Foundation Behaviors: A supply of variable reinforcers and a strong bridge are helpful.

Request: Some behaviors such as stay naturally lend themselves to either visual or auditory signals, or both.

Response: Animals asked to stay should freeze in position. In other words, unless you are not too concerned about your specific criteria, animals asked to stay while standing should remain standing and those sitting should remain seated.

Duration: Stays can be conditioned to extend almost indefinitely. In fact, I knew a professor who put his dog in a stay position outside the building as he went off to teach class for a few hours each day. Try as I might, the dog ignored my attempts to interact with it. One way to maintain a great stay like this is to avoid setting an upper limit to the duration of the stay. Ask for and reinforce a few seconds more than the animal's current criteria whenever possible. The chances for a bit more success are highly probable, unless you are also concentrating on one of the other components below.

Energy: Look for low intensity behaviors. Avoid reinforcing animals as they fidget, scoot, slouch, or appear otherwise distracted.

Frequency: This is probably not an important component to a stay, but avoid asking for the predictable, long stay, day after day. Mix it up by asking for several shorter duration stays once in a while.

Topography: As with training any behavior, when the complexity of the situation increases, it's important to temporarily lower other expectations such as the duration of a stay.

Reinforce: Teaching a stay is simple, provided the trainer uses proper placement of reinforcement. For most behaviors, animals typically are reinforced for being near the trainer. This is particularly true when we offer food rewards. But this tendency is counterproductive to teaching the stay since you're asking the animal to remain behind while you, the source of reinforcement, leave the area.

To counteract this inevitable imbalance of reinforcement, keep the following in mind while teaching a stay. Limit bridging an animal for the stay, which actually recalls them to your location to receive further reinforcement. That is precisely what they want to do and exactly what you are asking them not to do. Instead, *the trainer should often return to the point of the stay and reinforce* the animal for holding its position. It also doesn't hurt to have a good throwing arm to deliver the reward! In addition, use some reinforcers that have been preset and hidden behind or near the animal's location. This may help to teach the concept that reinforcement comes from many sources (not just your pockets) including the immediate environment, so there's no need for the animal to split from the stay to find you.

Concurrent Behaviors to Avoid: Behaviors best reinforced while the animal is near the trainer, such as a heel or name recall, should not be combined with the stay.

Stay Calm
How do I shape my animal to be always calm and attentive?

Objective: To teach animals to respond without anxiety, vocalizations, forceful, or obnoxious behaviors the majority of the time. To help them understand the difference between playtime and the other 23.75 hours of the day.

Desensitization Required: Desensitization will play an ongoing role in teaching an animal to be calm and attentive. It's a lifelong process.

Suggested Foundation Behaviors: A variable supply of reinforcers is helpful.

Request: Except when we request high energy or play behaviors, most of us would prefer to have animals that spend most of their time quietly making their way through the house or yard, playing alone with toys, sleeping through the night, hanging with the family while watching TV, and so on. However, trainers often unconsciously let predictable events become cues for the animal that it's time for energetic play behaviors when they would probably prefer the opposite. For example, after a long day alone the dog hears your car pull into the driveway or the jingle of your house keys as you unlock the door. Understandably, the animal will be excited when someone comes home. The same thing happens when keepers drive the feed truck up to an exhibit. How the trainer reacts as he/she enters the home or exhibit will go a long way in determining whether the animal learns to respond in a controlled fashion or completely out of control. Events like your arrival or departure are common occurrences with predictable outcomes from the animal's point of view. Because animals quickly learn whether or not they will receive reinforcement when you come or go, these experiences can have a profound effect on learning. So trainers, pay attention to what follows next.

Response: Shaping animals that are relaxed does not mean you are creating lethargic creatures with low motivation—just the opposite. It's natural for an animal to respond with some energy as we arrive home. In fact, we'd probably be disappointed if they didn't show some interest in our comings and goings. However, upon arrival, trainers should allow some of the excitement to pass before finally reinforcing animals for lower energy behaviors. This will help avoid shaping inappropriate behaviors during highly predictable events or routines.

Duration: If trainers are consistent, animals will soon learn that calm responses get reinforced. As a result, animals will increase their display of calm responses over energetic ones. These behaviors will spill over into the rest of their 24-hour day if we pay attention to them. For example, back when he was a 100-pound puppy, my wife and I actively reinforced our shepherd mix to sit whenever anyone came to the house or pulled into the driveway. We were concerned that one unexpected energetic jump up onto my father-in-law, who walked with the aid of a cane, would result in a disaster. To further reduce the odds of the dog jumping on someone, we usually limited our reinforcement to only those times when all four of his paws were on the ground. This was an easy criterion for us to remember and communicate to visiting friends. An additional side benefit of this effort was an animal that tended to sit whenever something new or confusing happened around him, not just when people came to the house.

Energy: Calm animals can and will still have energy; they just know when to turn it on and off.

Frequency: Shaping relaxed animals is easy if we remember to pay attention to them during the down times that occur in between high energy playtimes, training sessions, and long walks.

Topography: Avoid creating predictable situations that communicate "time to be crazy." For example, go to the park and spend some of the time at the beginning, end, or both taking a nap, watching the world go by, or enjoying some other low intensity reinforcers like a back scratch.

Reinforce: One of the problems punishment trainers run into is trying to motivate a chronically punished animal. As a result, when they aren't punishing behaviors, these trainers will often try to prop up an animal's motivation by reinforcing "attitude" or "effort." Unfortunately, these animals often stay "up" and display inappropriate behaviors at inopportune times. This can be extremely annoying to watch, much less endure.

Similarly, new pet owners often make the mistake of continuously interacting with their new puppy in energetic, playful ways. When a new pet joins the family, this rambunctious play is cute and undoubtedly fun for all. But what happens in a few months when the puppy is now fifty pounds heavier, not as novel as it used to be, and you are running late for school or work? Suddenly, that incessant running or jumping all over your clean clothes isn't as much fun or cute anymore. Let's face it. No one likes a hyperactive animal 24-hours a day. Too bad nobody stopped to inform the dog that those behaviors you found to be endearing and reinforced when he was a puppy are no longer wanted or appreciated. Talk about being unfair to the animal.

This outcome can be prevented in a simple way: balance of reinforcement. Let's suppose you spend a total of 20 minutes a day on average roughhousing and energetically interacting with your animal. In that case, plan on spending about 40 minutes (total) reinforcing them for low energy, all-four-paws-on-the-floor type behaviors. Think about it this way—do you really want to become a cue to your new animal that it is *always* OK to be a nut? Calm, relaxed animals are no accident. Their success is the result of spending time with them while they are relaxed and reinforcing calm behaviors such as lying down, sitting, being quiet, sleeping, or playing alone with a chew toy. For reinforcement trainers, it's much easier to encourage a relaxed animal to become energized, than it is to ask a hyper animal to remain quiet and calm. The take home message is this: if you don't want a behavior such as jumping on you uninvited to occur when the animal is grown, do not reinforce this response when your animal is a small and cuddly puppy. Reinforcing only the behaviors *you* request from your puppy will help it grow up to be the good family member you want as an adult.

One way to avoid accidentally reinforcing inappropriate responses, such as whimpers that turn into a long whine or loud barking, or dancing around our feet that evolves into jumping all over us while our arms are full of groceries, is to ignore the animal for several minutes upon our arrival or prior to our departure. This will result in an animal that is less likely to associate their agitated behavior with all the little cues signaling that you are coming or going, such as putting on your coat or the jingling of car keys. Instead of reinforcing this kind of behavior, wait a few minutes for them to calm down before you acknowledge them whatsoever. In fact, make it seem like you never left at all—as if you were just in another part of the house. This logic can even be advantageous in potty training. Upon arriving home, you should actually wait a few minutes before letting your maturing animal out for a potty break. Unless you've been gone well beyond their normal limit, chances are if the animal has held it this long, it can wait a few more minutes. Doing this will help prevent you from accidentally shaping a hyper animal that knocks you down on its way out the back door to relieve itself.

Concurrent Behaviors to Avoid: None

Heel

How do I get my animal to walk by my side without pulling ahead or dragging behind?

Objective: To condition the animal to walk, stop, or run as requested beside the trainer with or without a leash in any situation.

Desensitization Required: The level of desensitization required will depend on the complexity of the situations to which the trainer intends to expose the animal. For example, it is much less challenging for a pet to learn to walk on a leash in its own backyard, than it is to learn to walk off lead at a dog park, while randomly encountering new animals, as well as unfamiliar sights, sounds, and smells. To succeed, trainers must ensure that desensitization is an ongoing process as the animal matures and graduates to more complex topographies. If the animal is currently unable to heel successfully on a leash in the comfort and familiarity of your home, it definitely won't succeed at the dog park. So, hold off for now!

Suggested Foundation Behaviors: Eye contact, hand targeting, name recall.

Request: On the surface, heeling seems to be controlled by a variety of cues or requests. We may say the word "Heel," and think that controls the response, but in reality, for most animals heeling begins with that first step we trainers take. Think about it. Do you hear people walking their dogs down the street saying "Heel, heel, heel..." with every single step they take? Do these same dogs keep walking on their own if their trainers stop momentarily? The answer is no. Thus, it is our own act of walking that ultimately controls the onset of a heel behavior, not some superstitious word we say at the start of our motion. For example, the sea lions I once trained were conditioned to walk by my side whenever I walked. If I stopped, they were expected to stop, if I ran, they did, too. If I started again, they would bolt with me as well, unless I requested them to "stay." By the way, we never used a halter or leash on these 500-plus pound creatures. Simple targeting and placement of reinforcement was all that was needed to teach them a reliable heel along side the trainer. In our case, the request for "heeling" was simply the visual cue of taking a step.

Now for smaller animals that may not have the training history or attention span of an experienced sea lion, a leash can provide a useful context that suggests "we're going walking, side by side." However, the leash is not an instrument with which to drag or be dragged by the animal! Think of it instead as a fragile, thin thread used only to remind the animal of the distance you would like between the two of you. If either one of you pulls on the thread, it will surely snap, and the behavior criteria will be broken. Thus, *a leash is merely a targeting tool* that happens to provide your animal with an additional layer of information and safety. The leash should provide physical control only if absolutely necessary to prevent injury in an emergency or in the event something unexpected happens, such as an aggressive dog suddenly approaches you or a vehicle races dangerously close by.

Response: Each step the trainer takes is a request for the animal to follow along side.

Duration: Heeling is really a series of steps. Each step is one behavior that requires reinforcement. Fortunately for us, most animals seem to be able to cut us some slack on this last requirement. But keeping the idea of "step, reinforce, step, reinforce..." in mind may help you to better maintain this chain of behaviors, resulting in a strong heel at the start, middle, and end of each walk, regardless of the duration.

Energy: As the animal learns to follow at your side, trainers should vary the speed of the walk/run. Avoid being predictable in your pace or destination. If animals can predict where, when, or how fast they are going, they don't need you to show them. This is often how the heel behavior breaks down, resulting in a tug of war. For example, if the animal seems to want to forge ahead of you, slow down. If it lags behind, speed up. Otherwise, they are shaping your behavior! The logic here is much like that first introduced in the name recipe on page 87. If the animal veers away from you in any direction, gently veer the opposite way. If you don't, you risk inadvertently reinforcing them for the criteria they are setting. Don't pull or jerk the leash. Instead, keep the path interesting and reinforce them for paying attention to changes in *your* pace and direction.

Frequency: Changing the pace and direction as you both heel together requires the animal to pay attention in order to respond correctly and thus to receive reinforcement. Success hinges entirely on the trainer's ability to make the journey variable and interesting. Remember to randomly stop, start, move slowly, move fast, change directions, and reinforce them for making the appropriate adjustment quickly to the changes you have set.

Topography: Once the animal can heel reliably in familiar environments, introduce more complex situations. Quickly reinforce animals for ignoring unforeseen environmental distractions and maintaining proper heel criteria. Then, consider taking them to the source of the distraction as an additional reinforcement for paying attention to you.

Reinforce: The majority of reinforcement should come directly from you or from discrete places in the environment to which *you take the animal.* To convey the behavior concept, trainers should reinforce animals for close proximity. Keep in mind that new and exciting reinforcements come in all shapes, sizes, and forms. As unappealing as that old piece of trash or fire hydrant may seem to you, it's like buried treasure to a species with a keen sense of smell. Remember, some species are built to forage for a living. Don't deny them these naturally occurring and often unavoidable, environmental reinforcers. Take them near it before they start pulling you there! Imagine how much more attentive your animal will be as *you* zigzag the two of you down the street going from new smell to new smell! Most importantly, once they've had a brief whiff, use primary reinforcement for turning their attention away from the source of the delectable odors. That way, they'll learn it is more advantageous to quickly scan and move on rather than drag you back to the source of the smell.

Concurrent Behaviors to Avoid: To strengthen the concept of "walk beside me," avoid shaping other behaviors during the same session that communicate reinforcement is contingent upon "being away from me." (See the next recipe called an A to B.)

A to B

How do I get my animal
to move from point A to point B?

Objective: To teach an animal to walk, run, fly, or swim from one location to another. This may include shifting their attention from one trainer to another, or simply from location A to location B under the direction of one trainer. In zoos, shifting animals from night quarters to their exhibit in the morning and back again at the end of the day has long been a pervasive challenge. In dog obedience training, the A to B, also called a go-out, may include running from a trainer to an undisclosed destination (e.g., straight, right, or left) until instructed to do something else such as stop, turn around, return to the trainer, or jump an obstacle.

Desensitization Required: Animals should be desensitized to the environmental conditions in which the A to B will be requested. For shifting animals on or off exhibit, in or out of a stall, or in and out of the backyard, this includes desensitization of the door opening or closing.

Suggested Foundation Behaviors: A supply of reinforcers, targeting, and a name recall are helpful. Other behaviors such as turn around, sit, stay, or jump that the animal might be asked to display during its A to B, are also beneficial.

Request: The cue to go from point A to B may be as simple as a pointed finger or extended arm. Many species can learn to discriminate directions. For example, the trainer points (or says) to the right and the animal moves to the right.

Response: Teaching the concept of going to a fixed location is best achieved when the behavior is initially taught in reverse. In other words, pick a location the animal will repeatedly be sent to—the B point. Then move the animal to different locations, or A points. Early on, the predictability of placing the reinforcement at a fixed B point allows the trainer at position A to move about, to send the animal from any location above, below, right, or left of position B. Training this way allows the animal to quickly generalize the idea of going to point B no matter what the environmental conditions may be or where the starting point is. It also doesn't require another trainer to be present at position B as long as reinforcement is already available there.

Once the animal understands the concept of "go away from trainer at position A," it's a simple matter to teach him to "find a trainer at any location B." In this case, the animal is asked, often by a visual signal such as a finger point, to find another trainer somewhere in the environment rather than go to a fixed location. For this behavior, the trainer at position B will then have to provide additional information (i.e., a second request) by presenting the animal with a target or if known, a name recall. This is necessary in order for the animal to know where it is supposed to end up. Depending on your training situation, you may be able to fade this second target or recall signal at position B to the mere presence of another person, provided there are no other people nearby to confuse the animal.

Duration: Like other behaviors worked at a distance, the time to travel from point A to B will largely depend upon the criteria reinforced by the trainer(s) involved. If you use boring reinforcers or complicate matters by punishing your animals, their responses will tend to be slow.

Energy: Trainers who reinforce speed will get it.

Frequency: This is probably not as important a component as the distance between positions.

Topography: Returning to a trainer or going to another requires trust on the animal's part. The world is an interesting place full of distractions, so be certain to make the trip to you or to some static location worth the effort.

Reinforce: To prevent animals from wandering in search of their own fun, avoid using predictable reinforcements at position B. Also, similar to the stay behavior, reinforcement placement is critical. Therefore, as you are teaching the concept of going from A to B in sessions, limit the reinforcement offered at position A. Think of it this way. Why should the animal be motivated to search for position or trainer B if all the fun is with trainer A?

Consistently shifting animals from point A to B ultimately depends on what happens at each position. For example, one of the challenges of shifting zoo animals is the predictability of going on or off exhibit. Animals learn quickly that going inside may mean staying inside until tomorrow. Some species may prefer to go off exhibit because that is often where most of the primary reinforcement is offered by keepers; others may refuse to go inside due to an imbalance of reinforcement that favors staying on exhibit or due to the threat of punishment by another member of the group (see "teamwork" example on page 112). If predictability is contributing to the problem, an obvious answer is to randomize when the animals are asked to go in or out and for how long they must remain in one location or the other. Fortunately, many zoo directors are beginning to realize the long term behavioral benefits of giving zookeepers more flexibility to temporarily shift animals off exhibit, even if that means briefly moving them away from paying guests during normal operation hours, as well as having the ability to reinforce animals both on and off exhibit.

Concurrent Behaviors to Avoid: Behaviors best reinforced when the animal is near the trainer, such as heeling, should not be taught along with this behavior.

Retrieve and Release

How do I teach my animal to retrieve objects without turning it into a game of chase?

Objective: To teach an animal to locate an object and quickly return it to the trainer.

Desensitization Required: The animal should be comfortable approaching the object and holding it in its hand or mouth.

Suggested Foundation Behaviors: A reliable A to B, name recall, sit, and a supply of conditioned reinforcers. Also, for objects that may be hidden from the animal, rather than something like a ball that is tossed out in plain view, it may be useful to have a modified A to B behavior that instructs the animal to move ahead of you. A super-motivated trainer can also add directional criteria such as "go left" or "go right."

Request: Simple retrievals may use the object or toy as the visual cue, but auditory cues may work as well. Many species can learn to differentiate among different types of objects based on size, shape, touch, color, smell, etc.

Response: Depending on the criteria level desired by the trainer, the animal should select the object and quickly return it to the trainer. You may also wish to shape the animal to hold the object in its mouth or hand until asked to release it. Thus, retrieving an object quickly consists of at least four less complex behaviors rolled into one! In other words, you'll need to approximate (and variably reinforce) the search, the selection, the return to trainer, and the release of the object. Early on, each of these approximations can and should be worked separately.

Duration: The more difficult the selection criteria such as choosing a scented article from among many unscented ones, the longer the animal may take to process the correct object. Animals that take a long time to discriminate among many objects may not completely understand what the criteria for selection is (e.g., scent vs. no scent). This may be a clue that trainers should simplify sessions to improve the animal's competence and confidence.

If part of the finished behavior is expecting the animal to hold the object until asked to release it, you'll need to practice just having the animal hold the object. So whether you're practicing the entire behavior or just sitting in front of the TV with your animal nearby, reinforce him for slightly longer hold times and for gently allowing you to take any object from him. It's important to vary the reinforcers offered and to give him something meaningful when he gives up any object.

Energy: Animals that understand which object to retrieve will display greater speed compared to animals that don't. Trainers who punish animals for choosing the wrong object only worsen response times. Why would any animal be motivated to quickly return if it's uncertain about which article to choose and convinced it will be punished for making a mistake?

Frequency: Animals will retrieve, and most importantly, return again and again all day long if trainers make it fun.

Topography: As with all behaviors, the more trainers vary the conditions in which the retrieval is requested and reinforced, the more reliable it will become.

Reinforce: Often, the biggest challenge to teaching the retrieve is getting the animal to release it to the trainer upon request, without turning it into a tug of war or a game of chase. To minimize this, it's vital to reinforce the animal for bringing requested objects back to the trainer. Sometimes the object itself, such as a ball, can be the reinforcer. But even in this case, it's a good idea to reinforce handing over the ball with other things. You can always give the object back, but at least get in a few reinforcements for dropping the object in your hand, at your feet, or whatever criteria you decide.

People are often surprised to learn that marine mammal trainers pay particular attention to reinforcing animals for allowing us to *remove* objects used as reinforcers from their habitat. This is especially true when trainers remove themselves from the animal's environment. Once animals, including powerful killer whales, develop a bond of trust with their trainers, they often don't want the trainers to leave. So getting into their habitat isn't the problem—it's getting out! This means it's critical to continue reinforcing the animal after giving up an object, or the exit of the trainer from the water. Don't let the release of an object become a predictable "end of reinforcement" signal.

Concurrent Behaviors to Avoid: Trainers working on scent discrimination behaviors (i.e., find the scented article among a group of objects) might want to temporarily avoid other retrieval work or play that is not dependent on teaching animals to select between subtle cues (e.g., scent vs. no scent). Despite some potentially confusing similarities, seeing a ball thrown and then retrieving it requires a different skill set than being pointed over to a pile of objects and using one's sense of smell to pick the correct object. Therefore, it's probably best to teach one at a time.

Jumps
How do I teach my animal to jump objects like those found in an agility course?

Objective: To teach an animal to jump a wall, bar, or some other obstacle.

Desensitization Required: Acceptance of the equipment and materials used to construct the high jump.

Suggested Foundation Behaviors: Depending on whether you have someone helping you in the session, an A to B point including the concept of direction (e.g., right or left), name recall, stay, and a supply of reinforcers.

Request: The signal to jump may be visual or auditory.

Response: One way to approach teaching animals to jump a tall obstacle is to first teach them to step over shorter obstacles. Begin by simply reinforcing animals for stepping over the bar without touching it as it is placed on the ground. Then slowly approximate higher marks and reinforce animals for not making any contact with the bar. Think about it. The criterion for a successful high jump is not to leap a pre-determined height; rather the criterion is actually to *clear the bar at any height without brushing against it* with any part of the body. The bar will never fall if they are only reinforced for not touching it.

How does this affect your selection of approximations? For one thing, avoid getting greedy. You should set the bar only as high as you think the animal is likely to clear it without nudging it. It doesn't hurt to remind them of the criteria (i.e., don't touch the bar) by lowering the bar by half or more at the beginning of these sessions, either. It's true that it will probably be easy for them, but your point is to focus on the "don't touch" component to the jump, not the maximum height aspect. Later, if you overestimate the animal's ability and it grazes the obstacle in any way, even if the bar doesn't fall, try lowering the bar in *future* sessions, not immediately in the same session. Reinforce with the bar at a lower height until the animal is reliably clearing the bar again. In fact, for the next session, use a bar height that the animal is *guaranteed* to clear, even if that means placing it on the ground again. The ultimate goal is not to train them to leap to a predictable specific height, which can lead to boredom and a degraded behavior. Rather, the goal should focus on teaching them to clear the bar, no matter what the level, within the physical limits of their species or breed. We don't want to teach them how to just barely make it over; we want them to soar over it every time.

Duration: Probably not a major component.

Energy: The higher the bar, the more energy needed to clear the obstacle. Be certain the animal is ready for a high intensity request before you ask for it. There is no sense in asking for a jump if they just woke up from a nap.

Frequency: Having several jumps in succession will probably lower the maximum height the animal can achieve, especially if the jumps are located close together.

Topography: Make certain the environment supports achieving higher jumps by providing the animal with adequate footing and a long enough runway to gain speed. Teach your animals to clear obstacles that are significantly higher in practice sessions than those required for competition or an audience. With all the distractions that can accompany new locations, competition trials, or shows, "game day" should always be easier, not harder, than rehearsal for the animals. Since my ability to reinforce animals in a show or competition may be limited compared to training sessions, I want to be certain sessions are reinforcing and that the criteria I teach them is far more than what will ever be requested in a complex situation, like a competition or show. This will help add to the reinforcement value of these more challenging situations when rules or show quality demand that trainers limit their use of meaningful reinforcers.

Reinforce: Since the point of greatest interest is the instant just prior to when they are midair over the obstacle, a strong bridge is vital. Look for and bridge the instant their bodies are still slightly pointed skyward as they begin to clear the bar. Avoid always bridging late when they are already beginning to point downward after clearing the bar. A well-reinforced bridge will allow you to selectively reinforce animals for clearing the bar without making any incidental contact with their bodies. However, at the completion of the behavior, be certain to make it worth their effort for exerting so much energy! Don't just click and move on. Also, avoid placing the bulk of reinforcement as though it comes from behind the animal. For example, if you send them on a jump away from you, avoid calling them back to you to receive reinforcement. Otherwise, it's like accelerating a car with your foot on the brake. Why would they be motivated to run quickly ahead if they learn reinforcement is going to come from you while you stand behind them? Instead, provide the reinforcement ahead of them to maximize their speed and hence their energy to clear the bar.

Concurrent Behaviors to Avoid: Possibly the name recall if the animal is to jump while running away from you.

Balance Beam

How do I teach my animal to climb up, walk, or run on objects like a "dog walk"?

Objective: To condition an animal to walk along an elevated narrow board, or any other unusual structure.

Desensitization Required: Touching and walking on an unusual, possibly slippery surface like a wood board.

Suggested Foundation Behaviors: A solid heel behavior on and eventually off lead.

Request: Typically the trainer moves along side the animal as it walks along the beam. But it's also a simple matter for the trainer to use a visual cue such as pointing to the beam or an auditory cue like saying "Beam."

Response: The beam is just an extension of a normal heel behavior. The stronger the underlying heel behavior, the better the criteria for the elevated heel. As with the heel, if the trainer accelerates, the animal should accelerate; if he/she stops, the animal should stop without jumping off the side.

Duration: There's no rush! Teach animals to stand on the beam by using large amounts of reinforcement while they're on the beam. The more relaxed they are while standing on it, the more competent they will be later on racing across it.

Energy: Build speed as competence increases. Animals should travel across the beam at the pace you set. As you increase criteria by increasing the pace, raising the height, or narrowing the width of the beam, be careful not to (positively) reinforce an animal's escape response off the high beam.

Frequency: Probably not a major component.

Topography: Begin by teaching the animal to heel on a board while it is placed firmly on the ground. Initially, use a beam that is *wider than required* to meet competition rules in order to quickly convey the concept that reinforcement comes only while animal's feet are on the beam. For timid animals, you may need to approximate one paw at a time. Then, alternate training sessions between using a narrow beam located directly on the ground to work on speed and using a wider beam slightly elevated to introduce the concept of walking on a height. Remember, as you approximate greater complexity with a higher or narrower beam, be sure to temporarily lower criteria expectations in other aspects of the behavior. For example, we can presume it's easier to maintain balance on a wider beam. So as training progresses, ask for a faster pace on the wide beam and a slower, more controlled pace on an elevated or narrow beam. In time, you can merge these approximations into a narrow balance beam behavior that is quick, confident, controlled and elevated. In fact, for those of you who like to compete, teach your animal to succeed on a beam width that is a few centimeters narrower and raised a bit higher (within reason for the species) than regulations require for competition. Why? If the animal confidently succeeds at greater criteria in practice sessions, think how easy competitions will seem!

Reinforce: The bulk of reinforcement should come while the animal is on the beam, not once it has exited the board. The goal is to teach animals controlled movements while on the beam. The more desensitized they are for just being on the elevated beam, the more sure-footed they will be moving across it, regardless of the pace requested by the trainer. Placement of reinforcement *while they are on the board* is critical to conditioning animals to readily approach the beam. Reinforcing them after they leave the board actually rewards them for leaving it behind. Unless the animal finds it so reinforcing and actually refuses to come down off the beam, the bulk of reinforcement should always come for approaching or being on the balance beam. This will minimize any accidental negative reinforcement for escaping the balance beam.

Concurrent Behaviors to Avoid: None

Teamwork

How do I teach animals to
get along in a group?

Objective: To teach animals to cooperate with the trainer and each other while in a group of the same or different species.

Desensitization Required: Teaching animals to succeed while in a group is an extension of the basic desensitization training previously discussed. Working with a group of animals is actually about aggression prevention. The truth is, many social species form hierarchies. Just because you haven't consciously reinforced a dominance hierarchy in your home doesn't mean animals haven't formed one. It is important that you observe how your animals interact with each other well enough to appreciate each member's relative rank within the group. You will then use this information as you plan how, when, and *in what order* to reinforce group members for cooperative behaviors. Relative rankings within a group can and do change frequently, so stay alert.

Suggested Foundation Behaviors: Low energy, easy to complete, highly reinforced behaviors such as sit, stay, name recall, and a supply of variable reinforcers including a strong bridge, are helpful.

Request: Every time we put one animal near others, we are making a tacit request that everybody in the group get along. In a very real sense, the presence of another animal is a cue to be calm, cooperative, attentive—social. Thus, every situation that includes more than one animal is a desensitization opportunity. These events encompass new experiences, unfamiliar animals, and strange locations. But they also include the most predictable or routine activities involving the same familiar group of animals, such as feeding, sleeping, playing, or getting attention from the trainer.

Response: Ideally, animals will learn to display, in a group setting, all of the behaviors they understand how to do when they are alone. Early group sessions should focus on completing simple behaviors such as sit and calmly receive reinforcement.

Duration: Initially, the length of time a dominant animal will respond cooperatively in the presence of other animals, especially as they receive reinforcement, may only be seconds. It is critical that trainers not exceed the dominant animal's current threshold for allowing other animals near while slowly approximating longer interaction times. Unlike teaching the individual behaviors we've discussed thus far, trainers can really mess things up in a hurry by overestimating what *each* animal is capable of, such as duration with or proximity to other animals, on any given day. This is because there are more participants in the session! Through their behavior, each member of the group is capable of introducing punishment (e.g., pain and injury) and/or negative reinforcement (e.g., escape) beyond the trainer's immediate control. Take your time and let past success, not impatience, drive your decision to increase the duration of future sessions.

Energy: Begin with low energy behaviors that have a strong reinforcement history that each animal can readily succeed at, such as "eat your own food from your own bowl," stay, or sit.

Frequency: Design sessions which ensure 100 percent success for each individual by keeping session length short and behavior requests to a minimum. It's better to conduct ten 30-second sessions with zero displays of aggression and lots of reinforcement rather than one five-minute session mixed with failure. Don't be greedy— a failed approximation in a group setting can set you and the animals way back, creating a bigger hole than when you started.

Topography: Approximate working animals as a group by adding one animal at a time. You'll also want to approximate bringing animals closer to one another. Avoid reinforcing animals for being alone or separating themselves from others. Use a neutral location whenever possible. In severe cases, you may need to approximate animals for being in visual contact with each other (e.g., separated by a fence) before you can bring them into physical contact.

Reinforce: The important thing to consider, whether you are training two animals together or twenty, is the order in which you reinforce these individuals. In the wild, social animals form dominance hierarchies—an efficient system of social order built largely on force or the threat of aggression (i.e., punishment) that facilitates the concept of "survival of the fittest." This is a great system if your concern is the survival of a species. However, most of us are more concerned with preserving the peace in our home, kennel, troop, exhibit, or herd than we are with conserving a species. Thus, contrary to popular belief expressed by many traditional trainers, you should not try to simulate a wild pack in your home by positively reinforcing one animal as it intimidates another. *Instead of feeding or reinforcing the most dominant animal first, as many punishment-based trainers advocate, trainers should reinforce the dominant animal last every time, and only for displaying cooperative responses.*

Not convinced? Consider which of the following situations you would prefer: 1) The dominant animal is reinforced last for displaying cooperative group behaviors.

This permits less dominant (e.g., fearful) animals to participate in the session or approach the trainer and/or food bowl without fear. 2) The dominant animal is not only encouraged but reinforced for growling, biting, chasing, being territorial, hissing, or otherwise injuring another animal or family member that simply got too close. Clearly, option one is the better choice. *Consistently reinforcing the dominant animal last teaches it that other animals (or people) pose no threat; the sight of other pets getting rewarded will become a cue that their turn is next!* Through a process of desensitization, less dominant animals (or people) can become conditioned reinforcers to the dominant animal. This approach works because, unlike typical conditions in the wild where food and other reinforcements may be scarce, there is no limit to reinforcement while under human care. Reinforcing the dominant animal last means the difference between creating an atmosphere of scarcity in which one must compete, fight, or even die, and creating one where reinforcements are plentiful for all.

So how do you reinforce the timid members while the dominant, potentially most aggressive animal is breathing down everyone's neck? Obviously, delivery of reinforcement is important. Since the order in which trainers should reinforce animals is determined by the relative rank of the animals involved in a session, lowest first to highest last, it's critical to select suitable reinforcements such as tiny, quickly consumed amounts of food. Avoid feeding large amounts of food at any one time that can be relinquished by the timid animal at the first sign of intimidation by animals of higher rank. In other words, don't set everyone's food bowl down, leave the area unsupervised, and expect all of them to know how to avoid getting into trouble. If necessary, feed smaller amounts at a time and reinforce pushy animals for letting the others eat. Feeding time is one of the most reinforcing (or punishing) moments of their day. So control everyone's access to food to prevent accidental shaping of aggression.

Reinforcement trainers don't deny the existence of social hierarchies exhibited by some species. We simply recognize that humans aren't ever going to be as strong, fast, or large as whales, lions, elephants, or *every* dog. Therefore, we'd better find a way of training them that transcends the underlying social order to ensure the success and well being of every group member, including us. Zoomility isn't about trying to be the alpha or pack leader to a species that is not our own. It is about shaping reliable, cooperative behaviors among humans and animals.

Concurrent Behaviors to Avoid: None. Teaching animals to calmly succeed in a group setting is a vital part of preparing animals for anything life with us throws at them.

The Doctor's Office

How do I teach my animal to remain calm during a veterinary exam, to clip its nails, or even to draw blood?

Objective: To teach an animal to remain calm and relaxed during veterinary exams including the collection of a blood sample from a species-specific site such as the leg, ear, or tail fluke. Many of the same logical steps can be applied to more common, less invasive, but potentially just as painful procedures like nail trimming.

Desensitization Required: Veterinary behaviors that create momentary discomfort are some of the most demanding behaviors that a trainer can teach an animal. They require a high degree of trust and precision between the animal and trainer that can only come from extensive desensitization training through positive reinforcement. Animals should be accustomed to the equipment used (e.g., syringe, clippers, stethoscope, etc.), protective barriers if any, and the number of people required (e.g., presence of veterinarian) to collect the sample. A variety of approaches have been developed to simulate the actual insertion of a needle, which is the instant at which there is the most discomfort and the point at which the animal is most likely to fail. These include: a gentle pinch at the site for species with fleshy skin, a light snap of a rubber band against the skin, or the slight pressure of a paper clip or finger nail at the site. Warning: blood collection should be conducted only under the supervision of a veterinarian. Proper sterile techniques should be maintained throughout all training approximations.

Suggested Foundation Behaviors: A relaxed "at rest" position that is species-specific. For example, standing in place for a rhinoceros, floating flat and belly (ventral) side up at the surface for dolphins, wings extended lying on its back with ventral side up for birds, or in a sitting or down position for dogs and cats.

Request: Drawing blood voluntarily from an animal is an extension of behaviors such as stay in position and desensitization to having its body manipulated. There are several additional steps to actually collecting a sample including: shaving the site in certain species, cleaning the injection site with alcohol, inserting the needle, pulling the plunger on the syringe, removing the needle, applying pressure to stop bleeding, and finally, calmly holding position until bridged and reinforced. Ultimately, each of these steps will signal the onset of the next.

Response: Few behaviors require the level of precision by an animal and trainer than drawing blood. Given the small body size of some species and their tiny blood vessels, even minute signs of muscle tension can mean the difference between success and failure. Thus, trainers must be certain all behaviors leading up to the actual moment of needle insertion are 100 percent successful. For instance, there's no sense in advancing the needle, with the obvious discomfort associated with it, if the animal won't lie perfectly still as you use an alcohol wipe.

Duration: Unlike most behaviors, the duration of a blood collection can vary from one attempt to another, even in the same animal. To help with this, trainers should reinforce extended stationing positions whether that means standing, floating, or sitting.

Energy: Animals should be reinforced for low intensity behaviors such as slow, rhythmic breathing, remaining motionless, relaxed muscles, and stress-free eye contact.

Frequency: Animals with a strong history of success can learn to give blood samples voluntarily as needed, even several days in a row. Amazingly, even animals that are showing signs of illness or have gone off feed have been known to successfully give blood upon request.

Topography: Given the difficulty for completion and the importance of success to an animal's health care, trainers should initially strive to simplify the environment as much as possible. As the animal progresses, small changes can be introduced, such as having companion animals in the vicinity or drawing blood on another animal nearby.

Reinforce: Selecting appropriate reinforcers to match calm behaviors associated with veterinary care, such as blood collection, is critical. Animals anticipating a loud whistle bridge or some other energetic reinforcer might be tenser than animals conditioned with soothing reinforcements. Clearly, a difficult behavior such as this should be met with the most effective reinforcers available for that animal.

Furthermore, due to the brief discomfort of the procedure, maintaining a voluntary blood draw (or any veterinary behavior) requires frequent training sessions. Aspects of the complete behavior, such as a calm tail fluke, wing, or paw presentation should be reinforced daily. For every approximation that involves an actual needle insertion, whether blood is obtained or not, trainers should conduct many more sessions to simulate and reinforce each step of the behavior, except the actual insertion of the needle.

Regardless of whether you are attempting to give an injection, draw a blood sample, or simply trim toenails, the potential for some discomfort is always present. Taking slow, deliberate approximations that encourage relaxation followed by lots of reinforcement can alleviate much of this. Trainers should always be mindful of the negative reinforcement that is inherent in these sessions. Be on the look out for avoidance responses such as increased muscle tension or withdrawing a limb, paw, or tail. In those instances, use an LRS until the avoidance behavior ceases. And, never console an anxious or fearful animal that backs away from you, the needle, or the nail trimmers. Instead, only reinforce them for approaching you and the scary instrument. Successful voluntary veterinary behaviors, especially those that may create brief discomfort, are the result of frequent desensitization sessions.

Concurrent Behaviors to Avoid: None

NOTES:

PART TWO

But *My* Walrus
Isn't a Clean Slate

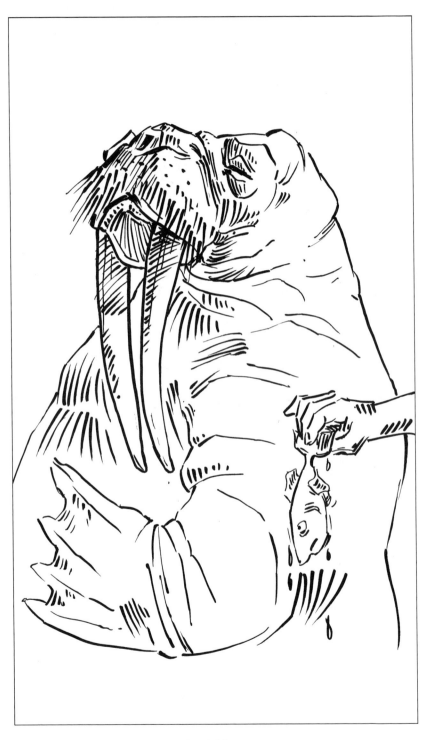

ZOOMILITY 601

For those of you with a pet that seems to have all sorts of problem behaviors, you might be wondering if the reinforcement-only approach can really work to improve your situation. After all, it's one thing to start fresh training a naïve puppy or kitten. But what about an older animal—one with a less-than-stellar history? Can adopting some zoomility of our own really improve the behavior of an experienced animal that has learned all sorts of unwanted, annoying, even dangerous behaviors because of past punishment, reinforcement, or both? No living thing is perfect all the time. Every animal will display something we humans find undesirable at one time or another. How a trainer responds will determine whether one unwanted episode leads to a series of failures or a lifetime of success.

Nowhere are the training stakes higher than in dealing with an animal with a history of destructive or aggressive behavior. The misguided but popular approach uses punishment to try to out muscle or intimidate hostile animals into submission. But what if the animal refuses to submit no matter how severe the punishment you inflict? Or, suppose you as the primary trainer are able to impose your will through force. How does that help anyone else in your home get along with the animal, especially when you're not there? In the end, if such an animal has to guess whether it should trust or fear you or anyone else, the odds are good that somebody will soon need a bandage. Sound extreme? Consider the story of a walrus I used to know.

This walrus was young and strong with a large number of behaviors under his belt. He tipped the scale at well over 1000-pounds and his tusks were about a foot in length and sharp, typical for this species. Behaviorally, his responses were usually crisp. He had only one problem—an incredibly low threshold for handling his frustration. Make the mistake of repeating the same request again after he refused it the first time and he'd probably charge you, leading the way with those nasty tusks. Conducting a body exam? Better be certain you know where he was desensitized to your touch and where he wasn't! Just because he was big didn't mean he was slow. Need to teach him a new behavior? Better not frustrate him by raising the criteria expectations too fast. Now with most animals, creating a small amount of frustration in your sessions by asking for slightly more criteria can be a good thing. A little frustration can lead to greater bursts of energy resulting in improved performance. Not so with this guy. Even a small increase of frustration had to be handled with the utmost care.

If there was any good news, it was his extensive and well-reinforced behavior repertoire. We never knew when he might drive one of his trainers backwards, threatening to plunge his tusk into a leg or pin one of us against a wall. Yet even when he was showing signs of aggression, we could count on him to reliably respond to previously reinforced requests such as dropping to his belly and lying completely flat in a behavior called a "trance." This reliability gave his trainers a number of safety options. If he showed indications of becoming aggressive to one trainer, another trainer or spotter could call his name to redirect him away from his current trainer. This redirection technique often helped diffuse the situation. Regardless, we always reinforced the behavior that was incompatible with him completing the aggressive response, such as dropping to the ground vs. raising his head, or changing direction vs. charging ahead. As this example demonstrates, requests for behaviors that are maintained only with reinforcement can reliably lower an animal's frustration and reduce the odds that aggression will escalate.

Although this walrus was prone to some of the most extreme and dangerous behaviors possible, he was also living proof that trainers don't have to respond to problems, even overt aggression, with anger or punishment. *As long as sessions are planned accordingly,* a little behavioral ingenuity and a history of positively reinforced responses can be used to redirect an animal from displaying unwanted behaviors to achieving successful ones. This approach allows us to remain reinforcement-only trainers while at the same time, to effectively reduce any undesirable behavior, including aggression. Speaking from personal experience, it can also save your life.

Besides, even if you wanted to, how could you dominate a one-ton walrus?

Using Positive Reinforcement to Change Course
Before the Collision

Assuming at this point any punishment trainers are still reading

Zoomility, they are probably scratching their heads in disbelief. Why would anyone offer "treats" to an animal that is showing any unwanted behavior, especially aggression? To the contrary, as we examine the walrus example more closely, we can see that this animal was *not* reinforced for being aggressive. In actuality, he was reinforced for choosing an alternative path instead of more severe aggression. By responding to the diversionary request, he chose a constructive behavior, which deserved to be reinforced. In the heat of the moment, this provided us a small window of opportunity to start things over (or end the interaction safely) and prevent a disaster.

As reinforcement trainers, our job is to acknowledge animals for successful behaviors we'd like them to display again and again. But what about animals that have learned to engage in unwanted, destructive, or even aggressive behaviors? Can we really teach them to behave in an entirely new way without resorting to punishment?

One tool at our disposal is the Least Reinforcing Scenario, or LRS. By controlling the animal's environment, which means controlling its access to sources of reinforcement, we can use the LRS to prevent strengthening unwanted behaviors accidentally. This allows the process of extinction to take over so behaviors that are no longer reinforced will eventually fade away.

In the interest of full disclosure, this raises a serious question or two. Does training with zoomility mean we have to endure repeated displays of unwanted behaviors until they are forgotten? Are we really limited to just waiting for poor behaviors to be extinguished through our non-reinforcement? Suppose we succeed in controlling all *external* sources of reinforcement. What if simply completing the undesirable behavior is all the reinforcement the animal wants? After all, engaging in behavior like aggression can be fun for the winner. So is the LRS our only tool to reshape a previously learned, undesirable behavior? Fortunately, the answer is no.

For all its effectiveness in preventing accidental reinforcement or worse, deliberate use of punishment, the LRS still occurs *after* the unwanted behavior has taken place. How much better it would be if we could make using an LRS unnecessary by preventing the unwanted behavior from ever happening! Luckily, there is a proactive technique to compliment the LRS.

When a trainer communicates by way of the LRS, he is able to show that a behavior that already happened was undesirable and will not be reinforced. So, to begin shaping new, successful behaviors, we need a training tool that lets us show the animal exactly what behavior *will* be reinforced in the future. Such a technique should enable a trainer to be proactive and take action at the first sign of trouble, before the unwanted behavior appears, and still without resorting to punishment.

For reinforcement trainers, that tool is called *alternate response training using differential reinforcement.* Differential reinforcement means we are going to very carefully choose what behaviors we're going to reward. Alternate response training uses delivery of this very selective and deliberate reinforcement to reward constructive behaviors in place of the ones we want to avoid. What constructive behaviors should trainers look for? In some circumstances, we may not care what other behavior the animal displays, as long as it doesn't, for example, bark incessantly. As a result, we may not be too particular about what behaviors we actually reinforce, so long as none of them include making any sound! This is called differential reinforcement of *other* behaviors or DRO.

Confused? Here's a common example of alternate response training in which we choose to reinforce animals for *any* response *other* than the problem behavior. Imagine you have a dog that howls whenever police sirens pass by. Since the timing of this environmental cue is hard to predict throughout the day or night, trainers might wish to immediately acknowledge their animals for displaying any behavior other than making a sound as a siren approaches. In other words, *at the first hint a siren may be approaching and before the dog starts to howl, the animal is reinforced while it does anything other than make noise.* Any silent behavior such as sleeping, lying down, or playing quietly with toys will work. Obviously, using DRO assumes that the *other* behaviors that you are reacting to are preferable to constant barking!

Differential Reinforcement of Other Behavior (DRO) means selectively reinforcing *any* behavior other than the one that is to be eliminated.

Sometimes, as was the case with the walrus, we may want to request a *specific* behavior. Usually we want to pick a behavior that actually *prevents* the animal from displaying the unwanted response. For example, asking the walrus to lie down was incompatible with him raising his head and driving his tusk into my leg. In those instances I used what's called differential reinforcement of an *incompatible* behavior or DRI. Similarly, having a fellow trainer call the walrus away was incompatible with it charging at me.

Differential Reinforcement of Incompatible Behavior (DRI) means selectively reinforcing behaviors that *prevent* the unwanted behavior from being displayed.

Need a more common example of how DRI can work for you? Imagine your dog has a history of jumping up on people as they come to the front door. To help reshape this response into something more desirable, you might try requesting the animal to "sit" well before the person comes near. In this case, you have requested the animal to complete a behavior that is incompatible with jumping up on the approaching person. If the animal complies, you should reinforce it for displaying a desirable behavior in a context that in the past had resulted in failure, not to mention an annoyed houseguest.

Using DRI assumes that the incompatible behavior you've selected has a strong reinforcement history. In other words, the incompatible behaviors you request must be highly reliable all the time, not something you hope will work when your life is at risk. If the animal is unfamiliar with your behavior request or if you have not reinforced the incompatible behavior very well in the past, the odds of successfully using DRI will be low. It's easy to see why. If the animal has to guess whether or not a response will be reinforced, it's not likely to choose the new option you are offering.

Differential Reinforcement allows you to diffuse a powder keg. Punishment lights the match!

Thankfully, our walrus reliably dropped to his belly without hesitation because this desirable behavior was reinforced frequently every day of his life. It was through reinforcement, not force, that we were able to safely redirect him from a path of destruction to one of success.

Quite honestly, if you've never been on the receiving end of a one-ton animal's aggressive behavior, the effectiveness of a well-timed DRI to divert it from hurting someone or something is nothing short of amazing, especially when it's your own neck you're saving! But don't let its usefulness fool you into using the same DRI over and over again in the same situation. When you find it necessary to use DRI repeatedly just to avert disaster, that "wall" you are hitting (figuratively and in my case, literally) is actually the animal trying to tell you something. The message is this: you'd better start paying attention and make some changes to your session planning before things spiral completely out of control. Consider whether your training sessions or approximations need to be simplified, the animal needs more desensitization training, the

Live or die by DRI. If you need to use DRI often, the animal is telling you that something you are doing needs to change.

animal is afraid, your reinforcements are inadequate or too infrequent, or there's more going on in the environment than you realize.

Are You Shaping a Bully?

Much of *Zoomility* has underscored the harmful, even foolhardy, side effects of using punishment, including the shaping of fearful, antisocial, and aggressive animals. But even positive reinforcement can play a role in teaching our pets annoying or unwanted behaviors, as well as aggression, when it's applied the wrong way. In many cases when this happens, the reinforcement was unintentional. Often, trainers simply fail to adequately control the environment by removing inadvertent sources of reinforcement such as food left over in a bowl or one chew toy left in a yard full of dogs. Our oversight makes it possible for animals to find their own source of reinforcement at the most inopportune times! To make matters worse, instead of using an LRS, frustrated trainers often react to their animals at the point of failure, which only serves to strengthen the unwanted response.

Sometimes, however, positive reinforcement is given intentionally when it probably shouldn't be given at all. It's that situation we need to address next.

As a zookeeper working with all sorts of animals, I believe it's important to know the natural history of the species I'm working with—how, why, and what it does for a living. But sometimes trainers overdo it. They take limited observations of animal behavior in the wild and suggest domestic pet owners try to apply the same ideas in their homes. For example, we all know dogs are social pack animals. As with any group of social beings, there's going to be a hierarchy in which some lead, some follow, and the rest fall somewhere in between. It's the alpha or leader which largely determines how the entire group functions. Among other things, the alpha *controls* who gets the choicest selection of food, where members sleep, and who gets to breed. So it's no wonder some people decide we humans should assume the role of the alpha "dog" in our own homes. After all, if it works in the wild, it ought to work in the home.

But consider this: in the wild, the alpha maintains control through constant force and dominance. This method is superb at ensuring the survival of only the fittest animals because it weeds out the sick, the injured, the old, and the weak. But these hierarchies can be extremely harsh, even cruel, to the individuals within the group. Even the bold, strong, and apparently invincible alpha will one day be replaced when it is no longer strong enough to maintain control.

Now translate that scenario to the human household. As alpha, the lead human must maintain constant, vigilant control through intimidation and force. How does this kind of dominance apply when there are children, grandparents, visitors, or other animals in the household? Even if you are willing to ignore the harmful effects of punishment, are you really determined to maintain social order through force every minute of every day? Suppose you are physically capable of pushing around your dog well enough to assert yourself as alpha. How does that make it easier for your family, including your dogs, to live together? What happens to the weaker members of your "pack" when you aren't home to control things? You can't assert yourself as alpha only when it's convenient or you have a point to make. If you choose to follow this path, it becomes a 24/7 job that only you can fulfill.

So what is it about a dominance hierarchy that makes encouraging one in our homes dangerous? Hierarchies teach animals to compete rather than to cooperate with one another, to test their own skills against the limits of their companions, to look for weaknesses, and to guard against potential threats from inside and outside the group. Again, this is a great system for survival in the wild, but not in the home where a pet's social companions are our children, other pets, our spouse, or the neighbors. Even if most pets submit to mom or dad as the alpha, all bets are off when grandma or junior comes near. Thus, attempting to train behavior and maintain order by being the alpha creates unsafe, unreliable, and unpredictable conditions for everyone in the family, including you. Plus, how can there be mutual trust if everyone in your pack is always on guard? Unfortunately, the widespread use of dominance and punishment training in our homes may explain why millions of pets bite their owners each and every year.

Contrary to what many pet experts would have you believe, having a social animal doesn't mean we have to imitate the inner workings of a pack. The bottom line is this: while it's true hierarchies do exist among some animals, particularly dogs, dominance hierarchies do not belong in the human home. To make sure you don't accidentally encourage a dominance hierarchy, never try to suppress unwanted behavior by punishment, and never reward any animal when it's attempting to intimidate others. As we've seen, everything about reinforcement is powerful, even its misuse. Be sure to use reinforcement carefully to shape greater cooperation among animals rather than increased dominance, fear, or avoidance. For more help on preventing and reducing bullying behaviors, reread the behavior recipe on page 112.

127

It's under control,
but are you?

ZOOMILITY 701

Admittedly, in animal training as in life, it isn't always easy to keep your cool.

One day, not long after my arrival at a marine mammal facility, I noticed that some debris had blown into the lagoon in an area not usually frequented by the animals. I decided to retrieve the article by slipping into the far side of the pool away from where the dolphins were currently engaged in a session "under control." Under control is one of those poorly coined but commonly used phrases in behavioral circles. It's supposed to mean getting and holding an animal's absolute attention no matter what, until *we* say otherwise. In truth, this is probably more wishful thinking than reality. If zoomility teaches us anything, it's this: trainers are often not in total control of the animals, the situation, or even their own reactions!

Which brings us back to my story. As I made my return swim to shore, a dolphin buzzed by me, then another, and finally another. By now I was swimming in front of a large beach area where the classroom portion of our children's program was in full swing. At this point, the dolphins were completely fascinated with the "stranger" in the water. They ignored their trainers at the far side of the pool, preferring instead to push and shove me like one of their toy boomer balls.

As a keeper, getting bumped around a bit by a large animal isn't all that unusual, even at the hands, or rather, the flippers of a dolphin. Despite the pop culture mystique, dolphins are big animals that are not, in fact, always smiling. Wild dolphins can be quite aggressive, even lethal with other species. Behaviors ranging from a gentle grazing by a tail fluke to the full chomp of some 80 plus teeth are an ordinary part of dolphin society. In general, behaviors that we humans describe as aggression such as staring, growling, stalking, pouncing, mouthing, pushing, and biting enable animals of every kind to survive the harsh realities of living in the wild. However, many of those pressures such as hunger and the need to hunt for food don't apply in a zoological setting. As a result, we're able to utilize unlimited reinforcement and lots of desensitization training to increase cooperative behaviors and minimize the frequency and energy of aggressive responses.

Yet even in trained animals, it's important to remember that aggression is normal. It's just not very desirable for most of us. Even with our best training efforts, those of us who choose to live, work, and play around any species may be on the receiving end of some of these undesirable behaviors from time to time. This is especially true when we are working with social animals like dogs or dolphins.

The real problem with displays of aggression, whether they are accidental, explicable, normal, infrequent, or mild, is that these behaviors can become self-reinforcing. As such, they can very easily escalate in duration, energy, frequency, and generalize to new topographies. Perhaps that's why people enjoy contact sports so much: there's a certain amount of pleasure in pounding the other guy. That sure seemed to be the case with the three dolphins that were taking increasingly energetic shots at mouthing my arms and legs and swatting me with their tail flukes. Eager to restore control (there's that word again) I asked one of the other trainers to signal for an immediate "recall." As demonstrated in the behavior recipe on page 87, a recall behavior is a highly reinforced, very common training tool used at marine mammal facilities. In this situation, a recall was used as a form of DRI (Differential Reinforcement of an Incompatible Behavior) that communicated to the dolphins "instead of using that trainer as a play toy, choose to come over here and you will receive reinforcement." Luckily for me, the animals eventually returned to their trainers long enough that I could climb out of the water and treat my superficial cuts.

Later, as the training team debriefed about what had happened, why it happened, and what desensitization work was needed to prevent this from happening again, several conflicting details surfaced. Some eyewitness accounts claimed that my immediate reaction wasn't simply to ask for a recall. Rather, I was told I asked for a "darn recall." One adamant staff member insisted I asked for a "gosh darn recall"—a claim I vehemently deny to this day. Either way, everyone agreed that at least I said "please." What I do remember quite vividly are the faces of about a dozen parents, one moment joyfully watching their kids as they prepared to meet a dolphin, and the next moment dropping their jaws to the ground as they witnessed a trainer getting munched right in front of them.

Should *Every* Animal Be Trained with Zoomility?

This zoomility story and the previous one of the walrus beg a much larger question: should every animal, no matter what its learning history or environment, be trained with positive reinforcement? Hopefully, readers caring for young or naïve animals, those "clean slates" waiting to be taught with only positive reinforcement, will answer "Of course!" But those of you who have an animal with a previously unknown, unsuccessful, or aggressive history may have trouble answering yes so quickly. That's understandable.

Sadly, many domestic animals have been so mistreated or neglected they pose a risk to other animals, people, and even themselves. Notwithstanding the power of positive reinforcement, it is much easier to prevent behavioral problems than it is to "fix" them once learned. If an animal has learned to display frequent and severe aggression, the possibility of those behaviors reappearing remains—forever. That said, I truly believe no animal is a lost cause.

However, that is *not* to say that all animals prone to severe aggression can be counter-conditioned with such certainty that they will be successful in any and all future situations or family home environments. In fact, most well-meaning pet owners are not equipped to rehabilitate *severely* abused animals with dangerously aggressive histories.

So where do you draw the line, and how do you know whether you can sleep at night with your decision to keep such an animal in your home? Perhaps the true tale of another animal with a checkered past will help show how everything we've discussed comes together.

Turning It Around for One Aggressive Dolphin

I once had the chance to work with a fantastic bottlenose dolphin. We'll call him Joe. When I first met Joe several years ago, this up and coming male was weeks away from joining our facility. Rumors about Joe's behavioral issues and learning history had been circulating among the local training community. So I decided to investigate them for myself prior to his arrival. At that time, Joe was living in a typical off-exhibit pool which had a cautionary wide red stripe painted about 2 feet out from the perimeter wall. I was quickly made aware of this line when my counterpart at the other facility chastised me for stepping too close to the poolside to see my own animal. While I was a bit puzzled by his vehemence, the larger point had been made—the stories about Joe's aggressive tendencies were real, and he was about to become my responsibility.

Actually, Joe's transfer to his new home was uneventful,

and his days instantly got a bit more enriching considering he was now in a natural seawater lagoon complete with native fish, sponges, other invertebrates, and five other male dolphins. For the first week or so, Joe was secluded from the other dolphins by means of a separate pool and underwater gate. To suggest he was "isolated" is a misnomer, since dolphins, like other marine mammals, are extremely acoustical in nature. Their amazing sense of hearing and wide array of whistles and clicks keep them in close "contact" with each other, even when spaced hundreds of feet apart. Being on opposite sides of a PVC fence was no barrier to communication. Our immediate goal was to focus Joe's attention on his new trainers and to assess his ability to display some basic behaviors. That first week gave him time to slowly and successfully meet his new social group without any risk to himself or the other dolphins.

Since Joe had been worked poolside with trainers standing completely out of the water most of his life, our biggest challenge was to safely, and as quickly as possible, introduce ourselves to his aquatic environment. Admittedly, the idea of getting into the lagoon with him was a bit scary, given his documented history of lunging out of the water and munching on trainers' hands and arms while on the supposed safety of dry land.

To minimize the likelihood of *trainer* errors that might lead to an aggressive response from Joe, only three of our most experienced people were initially approved to interact with him in any manner. In addition, since we were told a person's hand had been the frequent object of his attacks, in our early sessions we used a small buoy on the end of a short pole as his target. This prevented us from accidentally reacting to his aggression, in the event he became frustrated and swiped with his mouth, by keeping our hands out of his way. If we had reacted by quickly withdrawing our hands, as any sane person would, we would have negatively reinforced his aggressive behavior. The buoy target was used extensively anytime we were conditioning around Joe's face and for shaping longer stationing behaviors like maintaining contact with the target. Eventually, we were able to slowly and safely reintroduce the use of our hands as a target as he became increasingly reliable on the buoy. The more he was able to rehearse these simple behaviors successfully, the more frequently we could respond with reinforcement. Consequently, he was less likely to become frustrated or aggressive.

For all its benefits as a stimulating environment for animals, working in our natural seawater lagoon presented some challenges. Due to an irregular layer of rocks around the perimeter, there were only a few locations that lent themselves to working with the animal while the trainer was completely out of the water. We were concerned this limitation might make our sessions seem too predictable. While we wanted to create an environment of consistency, we didn't want things to become boring to Joe. So some of our earliest approximations were simple person-in-water desensitization sessions. These steps were necessary because at his former facility, Joe had learned that people in shallow water usually meant the start of some kind of veterinary exam. And since his previous trainers reinforced him from the safety of dry land, Joe was used to being alone in the water. The purpose of our desensitization sessions was to eventually introduce the concept that a trainer-in-the-water equals a good thing. But early on, we simply wanted him to ignore anything and anyone (namely me!) that might be splashing around in his new home.

Fortunately for us, Joe had a rather significant behavior repertoire upon which we could build. This included energetic behaviors like jumps and bows, as well as important veterinary behaviors such as body exams and taking voluntary blood samples. Unfortunately, these latter behaviors required trainers to be in close proximity to Joe. Not surprisingly, these were the same behaviors that had previously led to his most serious aggressions, such as taking a swipe at the trainer's hands or face. Still, the fact that he had already been taught several advanced behaviors meant we could make his training sessions variable, fun, and most of all, reinforcing to prevent boredom and frustration from setting in.

Before we could introduce him to his new dolphin companions or even the rest of the facility, Joe had to be able to demonstrate that he could reliably succeed at simple behaviors. One of the most basic was having him station on a buoy target in front of a trainer located on land while he ignored a trainer standing in the water near him. Once that was accomplished, we raised our behavior criteria expectations by pointing him over to the person standing in the water to receive his reinforcement (see A to B behavior recipe on page 103). In the beginning, the trainer in the water only offered reinforcement for responses requested by the land-based trainer; trainers in the water did not request behaviors of their own. Our goal was to help Joe associate his successful responses with reinforcement coming from the person in the water. Now, instead of seeing a trainer in the water as something aversive, as was probably the case at his former facility, we needed people in the water to become a conditioned reinforcer for Joe.

There's no denying the tension I felt the first few moments I stepped into the water and Joe sank below the surface to scan whatever had just entered his pool. Never mind the times he split from his station to check out my toes while I was floating in ten feet of water. But at no time did I have the sense that our approximations overestimated *his ability at that moment* to remain calm. If I had, we wouldn't have requested these more difficult approximations because that would have set him up to fail, not to succeed. I may have a tendency to rush things, but I am not stupid.

This is not meant to suggest that we didn't have an occasional setback. Years of animal learning and rehearsing aggression cannot be wiped away without a trace in a short time. There's always a probability, however low, that any previously learned behavior will spontaneously recur. Given that he was largely unknown to us, we were bound to stumble across a problem or two, as was the case when we placed our hands too close to his face or extended the duration of training sessions past his current limit. Yet, even with a few setbacks, our plan never wavered. We were committed to using the 3R's to create a consistent training environment that fostered clear communication, specific behavioral goals, and realistic approximations. Each session was designed to match the daily ebb and flow of Joe's interest, motivation, and skill set. In the event he didn't achieve a planned approximation, we didn't respond with "No" or other forms of punishment. How could we, even if we wanted to? Instead, we reinforced him for calmly accepting the LRS after any response that was below criteria. When it looked like his responses might be spiraling downward, we relied on DRO/DRI (reinforcing other or incompatible behaviors) to help him choose success over failure. Of course, we offered plenty of fun reinforcers for a job well done, and as a result, Joe soon became more successful, as his behavior demonstrated.

Within two months, he had safely met his first guests while they all stood in shallow water next to him. Not only was he able to engage in the behaviors he already knew, but he also learned new ones while in the presence of these guests. Furthermore, encouraged by another month of reliable success, we raised the stakes by incorporating Joe into deep-water interactions with guests floating relatively far from the shoreline. During these months, he also showed considerably fewer indications of becoming aggressive during those all-important veterinary behaviors, including voluntary blood sampling. What's more, he became increasingly comfortable with hands moving and working closer to his face. He adapted so well that by year's end he was able to offer a voluntary stomach tube sample.* For most dolphins, this isn't much of a challenge to learn. But for an aggressive, hand-sensitized animal like Joe, it required a great deal of trust between both of us. That kind of trust is possible only with positive reinforcement training.

Despite his history, Joe is a great animal. Time and again I've found that the most challenging ones are often the most fun to work with, in part, because they have the most potential to improve. To this day I miss working with him. There's something about working with an animal that others have already written off. To be sure, his past learning still presents many roadblocks, but as the saying goes, nothing worth having is easy. Still, I often wonder how much more success he might have achieved if it wasn't for all the trainer mistakes early in his life, plus the ones I no doubt added to the mix. What I do know for certain is that everything in *Zoomility* really works...the proof is in the results!

Joe's example illustrates how even animals with severe behavioral problems can be conditioned to be more successful using only positive reinforcement. With Joe, it took incredible effort by experienced trainers to reduce the aggressiveness brought on by years of practice and compounded by countless trainer errors. And yet, none of this was his fault. It was ours. As with all pets or wild animals under human care, they learn and do what we teach them. Part of caring for animals then, whether they live in a zoo or in our homes, is accepting total responsibility for their behavior. Once we can do that, any anger or frustration we sometimes feel about their behavior in the normal course of a day or training session easily fades away.

In Joe's case, the memories of his early aggression and other undesirable behaviors will always be with him to some degree. Even with only positive reinforcement training ahead of him, he may never be quite as reliable as an animal that didn't experience many years of rehearsing undesirable behaviors like aggression. Those earlier learning events still lurk in his brain waiting for some trainer to make a mistake. Yet with experienced reinforcement trainers working with him, the odds for greater success and less failure or aggression are in his favor. So regardless of their learning history or whether they have been mistreated, all animals should be trained with only positive reinforcement. If we are willing to adopt a little zoomility, turning an animal like Joe from a path of severe destruction to one of success *can* be achieved through positive reinforcement.

However, not every family or home situation is equipped to deal with the challenges of an uncooperative, antisocial, destructive, or dangerously aggressive animal. Taking on such a challenge requires the will to completely control the animal's reinforcement environment 24 hours a day. It means having the conviction to refrain from using punishment,

---

* This is a common veterinary behavior that's possible because unlike humans, dolphins lack a gag reflex. The procedure requires the dolphins to allow us to voluntarily pass a flexible half-inch tube into their first stomach chamber to collect a fluid sample. Animals are taught to remain motionless as the tube is passed with their mouths open and their relaxed bodies floating vertically in the water. The sample is then analyzed under a microscope as part of a comprehensive preventative medical plan.

even if learning from pain and fear are all that the animal has ever known. Most of all, it demands the patience to measure success in small steps, not necessarily by leaps and bounds. Understandably, these challenges represent more time and effort than many families can afford. So if you're dealing with an aggressive animal, or one with a history of undesirable behaviors, the real question to ask yourself is: do you and all the people around you have the skills, space, time, and commitment to train this animal?

Fortunately, Joe's tale is an extreme example. While each of us has made some training mistakes over the years, most of our pets have an incredible tolerance for dealing with them! As a result, few of us have to deal with problem behaviors as severe as Joe's. Yet, the same easy to use reinforcement tools that helped us turn it around for one dolphin can help you improve your pet's responses. Our pets deserve our best. So before you give up on them, give zoomility a try.

Getting Back to a (Mostly) Clean Slate

Using Joe's story as the model, here are some general guidelines to help get your animal's behavior back to a mostly clean slate. True, there's always a chance those old memories may pop up from time to time. But the more you can create the conditions that foster future success, the lower the odds that those unwanted behaviors will return.

First and foremost, reinforce more often. The reason is plain and simple: you must stop taking all of their desirable behaviors for granted. By rewarding their constructive behaviors more often, animals will have less time and motivation to engage in unwanted behaviors. So learn to reinforce frequently throughout the day and night—not just when you feel like it, but when *they* need it most.

The best way to help your pets understand what you don't want them to learn is to show them what you do want them to learn!

In particular, get in the habit of acknowledging them for displaying useful behaviors that are the opposite of or incompatible with known problem behaviors. For example, are they initially calm and quiet as a neighbor walks up your driveway to say hello? If so, don't ignore your pets as they happen to succeed—help them and yourself by reinforcing their friendly, tranquil, sitting response as the neighbors approach. In other words, don't wait until *after* your dogs start barking or jumping to react.

Second, use everyday activities to seek out opportunities to desensitize your pets. For example, if your pet sleeps through the phone ringing or a distant thunderclap, great! Reach over and give it a meaningful pat on the head or a favorite treat. Desensitization training does not need to be difficult or time consuming. It *does* require us to be aware and ready to reinforce whenever our pets don't react to potentially scary things, events, or sounds that may randomly appear in their environment. Clearly, the dolphins I encountered at the start of this chapter needed more desensitization training to prepare them for whenever trainers entered their environment in unusual locations.

Third, identify the behaviors you consider to be a problem and write down all of the conditions that usually precede them. What cues are linked to the unwanted behaviors? What happens as a result of the unwanted behavior? Is the animal accidentally reinforced? In the past, has it learned to avoid some form of punishment from you, another animal, or the environment? For example, let's say your dog is afraid of thunder. You might notice increased nervousness as a storm approaches. Your dog might also whine and beg to be held when a storm is near. What do you do when this happens? If you pick up the dog and try to soothe it, you may be unintentionally reinforcing its display of fear. After all, if you're going to give it attention, all the more reason to act afraid! Keeping track of details such as these will help you better understand why animals engage in certain undesirable behaviors. With that knowledge, you can then plan future training sessions designed to reduce and perhaps eliminate those problem behaviors using only positive reinforcement.

A key ingredient here is to prevent their failure. Every time animals rehearse an unwanted behavior, they get better at doing it. It's important to provide structure for them day and night in a manner that reduces the odds that they will engage in problem behaviors. One way to do this is for you to completely control access to all the sources of reinforcement in their immediate environment. For example, put items away that, if left on the counter or floor, might be too tempting for your pet. Learn to close closet and bedroom doors behind you to prevent pets from gaining access to your things. If necessary, use crates and kennels to prevent access to other parts of the home or yard; just be certain to keep those enclosures fun and the amount of time they are kept inside variable!

Ask yourself who's really at fault if your favorite leather shoes get chewed on—the puppy who just needs to teethe, or the human who didn't put them away?

It's not enough to create conditions that help prevent the display of unwanted behaviors. You'll also need to plan learning sessions that actively encourage the sort of behaviors you do want to see, while at the same time discourage the ones you don't. As we've discussed, the best training sessions are ones that are simple, that are easy for the animal to understand, and that practically guarantee your pet's success. If you're stumped about what behaviors to teach your pet in place of the problem responses, go back to Part One of *Zoomility*. Use the 3R's (Request, Response, and Reinforce) along with the supplied behavior recipes to begin shaping calm, desirable foundation behaviors. The more you reinforce a pet to sit, stay, or heel, the more likely he'll do just that when you need it most. There's no better way to help animals adjust to complex situations than by giving them a new foundation of behaviors from which they can choose to succeed.

If your pet tends to be overly energetic, focus on teaching and rewarding calm behaviors like sit, heel, stay, and down.

It's inevitable that we will sometimes overestimate a pet's ability to succeed, which means failure is bound to happen from time to time. When it does, learn to ignore its behavior by responding with the LRS. In time, behaviors that are no longer reinforced by you or the environment will undergo extinction as they fade in frequency, energy, and duration. However, in the interest of full disclosure, don't be surprised if the unwanted behavior gets worse temporarily before it gets better. I'm not kidding. Things may indeed get worse with the consistent use of LRS before they get better. The reason is frustration. Frustration occurs when animals and people, for that matter, don't get the reinforcement they've come to expect. Sometimes frustration is a good thing—it can lead to greater criteria. For example, animals that don't get bridged for a high jump for which they've been previously reinforced might try a bit harder by running faster and gaining a little more height over the bar (i.e., increased energy) or they may repeat the same jump (i.e., increased frequency) thinking that will gain them access to reinforcement. In fact, this is precisely what trainers hope will happen as they try to teach a *desirable* behavior or raise its criteria.

However, an undesirable response undergoing extinction will also create some degree of frustration for an animal. As a result of this frustration, some animals will display the unwanted response for longer duration, with increased energy, or more

Reinforcement is like payday. Imagine how frustrated you might be if your paycheck didn't show up on time.

frequently in search of the expected reinforcement. In some cases, animals will even start to offer other behaviors at random, in hopes of receiving the reinforcement they've learned to expect. This too is normal. But if trainers lose their patience and accidentally or intentionally reinforce these frustration responses by reacting to them, the problem behaviors will likely worsen! It is vital for trainers to see the extinction process through to its completion or the unwanted behaviors will not only reappear, they will get stronger. When you're attempting to eliminate a previously reinforced behavior through extinction, use the LRS and do not react to the burst of energy that may follow. Usually, once the animal's frustration response has played itself out over several sessions, the duration, energy, and frequency of the unwanted response diminish quickly.

Finally, if it appears your animal is about to engage in that familiar, yet undesirable behavior, try using DRI/DRO to redirect them back onto the path of success. Of course, DRI/DRO requires that the animal knows how to do some useful behaviors like sit or stay really well. But the technique does work as long as we continually do our part to reinforce these simple behaviors, while also refraining from ever using punishment. This rule also includes any other people who may be around our pets. Friends, family, strangers, and neighbors can have a huge effect on our pets learning and behavior. Just be sure to inform friends and family what you expect of them whenever they come in contact with your pets.

It All Comes Down to Zoomility

As we saw with Joe the dolphin, the process for improving your animal's behaviors is the same as it is for building them in a naïve animal. In both cases, we absolutely desensitize, but for animals with past failures, we probably need to do it more often each day. In both cases, we proactively control our pet's environment to prevent accidental reinforcement of unwanted behaviors; for pets with problems, we just have to be more diligent about it. For all animals, we must create fun and easy to understand training sessions using the 3R's to shape constructive behaviors without resorting to punishment; for animals with issues, we may have to simplify and reinforce things a bit more to overcome any past unpleasant memories the animals may have.

In all cases, we train using simple and realistic approximations. Responses are measured precisely in terms of duration, energy, frequency, and topography. And by offering interesting and variable reinforcements for the criteria we seek, we generate conditions that help animals to succeed, not fail. When mistakes do occur, it is our responsibility. We use the LRS to ignore their incorrect or undesirable behavior, even mild aggression. No matter how tempting or easy it may be to react with punishment, we never give in. Each training session is a fresh start—we never hold a grudge. Whenever possible, we use differential reinforcement (DRI/DRO) to get animals back onto a path of success *before* they fall short. We don't practice failure. And finally, with a little zoomility, we commit to putting their interests above our ego—enabling us to trust and have fun with our animals and they with us. And isn't that the reason we brought them into our lives in the first place?

In closing, I wish for you and your pets the kind of training success and joy that a zoo career has given me. Try not to take things too seriously, and remember to reinforce more, request less, and punish not at all!

Epilogue for Joe

Some time after leaving that marine facility, I had the good fortune to swim with Joe again. Happily, his hand swiping and other aggressive behaviors had continued to fade. Plus, his stomach tube behavior had become so dependable that his trainers can now pass a fragile and quite expensive fiber-optic scope down his esophagus for routine endoscopic exams—simply amazing! Joe continues to meet guests in creative, fun-filled sessions that are designed to ensure his success, not boost the trainer's ego. Still, with his learning history, I have no illusions that the journey will be as easy for him and his trainers as it is for animals taught to be winners from day one.

Fortunately for Joe, the people who provide his care do train with zoomility. As a result, each time he is positively reinforced for success, the odds of those old unwanted behaviors resurfacing diminish just a little bit more. His tale proves it's never to late to learn, or train, how to win.

141

LITERATURE CITED

1. Blanchard, Ken, Lacinak, Thad, Tompkins, Chuck and Ballard, Jim. (2002). *Whale Done!* The Free Press. New York, NY, 12, 25-49.

2. Ramirez, Ken. (1999). *Animal Training: Successful Animal Management Through Positive Reinforcement.* Shedd Aquarium, Chicago, IL, 45.

3. Kazdin, Allan E. (2000). *Behavior Modification in Applied Settings.* Sixth Edition. Brooks/Cole Publishing Company. Pacific Grove, CA, 26-51.

4. Pryor, Karen. (1999). *Don't Shoot the Dog.* Revised Edition. Bantam Books. New York, NY, 37-48.

5. Scarpuzzi, Michael R., Lacinak, Clinton T., Turner, Ted N., Tompkins, Charles D., Force, David L., Kuczai, Stan A. (1999). The Use of the "Least Reinforcing Scenario" in a Proactive Training Program in *Proceedings of the 27th Annual Conference of the International Marine Animal Trainers Association.*

Additional Resources

Chance, Paul. (1999). *Learning and Behavior.* Fourth Edition. Brooks/Cole Publishing Company. Pacific Grove, CA.

Behavioral glossary on www.IMATA.org.

Animal Behavior Management Alliance (www.theABMA.org)

ABOUT THE AUTHOR

Growing up in Cleveland, Dr. Grey Stafford started his zoological career as a marine mammal trainer at a place called SeaWorld of Ohio. For nearly 20 years, he has cared for and trained a variety of birds, mammals, and reptiles. Stafford completed his doctoral degree in reproductive and environmental physiology at Kent State University, where his research focused on New World primates. As Director of Conservation for the Wildlife World Zoo in Phoenix, he actively promotes wildlife conservation and positive reinforcement training through weekly televised segments in Arizona and contributions to programs such as *The Ellen DeGeneres Show, The Late Show with David Letterman, The Tonight Show with Jay Leno, Larry King Live, Martha Stewart, Good Morning America,* and *Extra*. He also posts a regular pet training column on Belo Corporation's website mysweetconnection.com. Stafford has been an invited speaker for national conferences including the Association of Pet Dog Trainers (APDT) and has co-authored award winning presentations and publications on animal behavior training techniques.

Stafford currently serves on the editorial advisory board for the International Marine Animal Trainers Association (IMATA). He is also a professional member of the Association of Zoos and Aquariums (AZA) and the Animal Behavior Management Alliance (ABMA). He currently lives in Arizona with his wife Karen and their own ever-changing "zoo."

NOTES: